How to Think and Design in the Third Dimension

Paul Jackson

T0385193

Laurence King

Contents

1

2

3

Symmetry on the XYZ Axes   87

4

Exploring Wider Concepts of XYZ Symmetry   125

Introduction

Look around you. You are in a space with height, breadth and depth. You can look up and down, left and right, forwards and backwards. These three dimensions are so ubiquitous that we rarely consider them as we go about our lives. A world without height, breadth and depth would be a world in another universe.

Clearly, then, everything we design and make occupies a part of this three-dimensional space. So here's the big question... why do we so rarely *think* and *design* in three dimensions? 'What?' you might mutter with disdain, looking at the many three-dimensional designed objects around you. 'Of course we think and design in three dimensions!' I would argue otherwise. In most cases, we think and design *flat*, in two dimensions.

For almost forty years across Europe and into North America and Asia, I have taught students from many design disciplines, from fashion to architecture, from jewellery to ceramics, professionals too. To my surprise, it became apparent that almost everyone designs three-dimensional objects as a series of flat pictures, taken from the front, from the back, from the top and from the side/s, rather than designing a three-dimensional object as a single three-dimensional entity.

So, using my students as unwitting laboratory mice, I designed a series of paper-folding exercises that tested their ability to think and design in the third dimension. Not surprisingly, I found their abilities were generally underdeveloped. Encouragingly, when they were given hands-on exercises to simultaneously relate the front of an object to the top, to the left side, to the base, to the right side in a fully three-dimensional way, their ability to think and design in the third dimension improved dramatically. A key element here was the use of three-dimensional symmetry, meaning: whatever happens along the X axis must also happen along the Y and Z axes.

This book is a collection of those exercises, tested on my students and selected for their usefulness. If you work your way through it, making as many examples as possible, your ability to think and design in the third dimension will likewise improve.

The benefit of this way of thinking is that it will literally open a new dimension to designing. No longer will such concepts as 'plan view' or 'side elevation' have any meaning. An object will be conceived in three dimensions, not as a series of plans and views. The three-dimensionality of your work will improve, making it visually richer, more interesting and more personal to you. The bottom line is that you will become a better designer.

Curiously, an object conceived in this way is very difficult to photograph so that its structure can be understood from just one camera position – a consequence, perhaps, of trying to depict a 3-D concept with a 2-D image. The solution for the book has been to include numerous QR codes that link to short movies, showing the structures rotating on a turntable. Only when rotating can their three-dimensionality become fully understood.

With careful study, the exercises in this book will teach you to think and design in the third dimension, increasing the sophistication and visual interest of what you design. Some of the constructions will seem like puzzles. You may find yourself muttering, 'If this unit goes here, then the second unit must go there...but then, where does the third unit fit?' In time, these conundrums will become quicker to solve, because you will be improving your ability to think three-dimensionally.

This book is also an excellent primer for teachers from elementary schools to university, who teach three-dimensional geometry, basic form (shapes) and versions of craft/design/technology curricula, and who are looking for simple, ingenious, aesthetic, inexpensive and quick ideas to teach.

I hope you enjoy the book, and that after making *making* MAKING, you will go wild using your new skills of thinking and designing in the third dimension.

How to use this book

The book is written like a novel, with a beginning, a middle and an end. Just as you would not read the chapters of a story in a random order, this book should not be read by flicking forwards and backwards, making the projects arbitrarily. Instead, please read the chapters in sequence. By doing so, you will come to understand, step by step, how to think and design in the third dimension.

But don't just read; don't just look! You should *make* as many of the projects as possible. Only by making will you become comfortable with thinking in the third dimension. Hands-on is always the best way to learn. When we make, we understand, but when we look, we have only the knowledge. Knowledge can be forgotten; understanding cannot.

Some of the projects will be time-consuming to assemble. That's a good thing. You will need to understand how each unit relates to the others using the principles of 3-D symmetry...and this may take a little time to comprehend and apply. However, this thinking time is very important, because it is the time when you are learning a new skill. It may be helpful to think of the projects as puzzles, as constructions to be assembled slowly and patiently. Don't give up too soon. The answers are there when you think in three dimensions.

In short, the more thinking you do and the more projects you make, the more you will learn from the book.

Materials and equipment

MATERIALS

All the examples in this book have been made with 190gsm card. If possible, buy the card in A4 or A3 pads (or, in the USA, ALS or Legal size), rather than in large sheets. It will be more expensive per square unit to buy pads of smaller sheets, but they are much easier to store without damage and much easier to cut if you have a small work area.

If you cannot find card of this exact weight, card in the 160–220gsm range is a good weight to use, because it gives not only stiffness and strength to a structure, but also a degree of flexibility. This is sometimes necessary when overlapping or interlocking adjacent units, when the card may need to bend and tuck.

Card that is thinner than this weight range will have limited strength, and card that is thicker will feel clumsy and unyielding. That said, some of the structures can be successfully and aesthetically made with thicker card, board, carton and even wood, metal and plastic.

Colour plays a very important part in understanding the three-dimensional symmetry in a structure. Thus, the constructions in this book are coloured not for eye appeal, but because the distribution of colour helps the reader to understand the structures with greater clarity. For this reason, you are encouraged to use a variety of coloured cards, not just easy-to-find white card.

EQUIPMENT

You will need:

- Hard pencil (2H), eraser and pencil sharpener

- 30cm (12in) and 15cm (6in) rulers

- A4 or A3 cutting mat (or larger)

- Good craft knife or scalpel, with
  a generous supply of blades

- Paper glue

LIGHTING

Your making experience will be significantly enhanced if you can work using natural light from a window positioned in front of your table. Artificial light – especially fluorescent light – can quickly tire the eyes. So, if you can, rearrange your working space – or even move to another place – to be near a window.

Further, the softness of natural light makes your work look more aesthetic, makes you want to work more and generally increases a sense of mindfulness.

Finally, any form of dominant top lighting should also be avoided. Top lighting minimizes the shadows across your work, making it look unnaturally flat when you are trying to maximize its three-dimensionality.

Symbols

Valley fold

Mountain fold

Cut

Glue here

Align the dots

How to cut and fold

CUTTING

When the shape is drawn, the next step is to cut it out. This must be done with precision, which is why you are recommended to draw with a sharp 2H (hard) pencil. This grade of pencil will create a pleasingly narrow line that will become the exact path of the cut. A softer or blunt pencil will create a wider, blacker line and, consequently, an inaccurate cut.

If you are cutting the card by hand, it is important to use a good-quality craft knife or, better still, a scalpel (above left). Avoid using the most inexpensive 'snap-off' craft knives, since they can be unstable and dangerous. The stronger, chunkier 'snap-off' knives are more stable and much safer. However, for the same price you can buy a scalpel with a slim metal handle and a packet of replaceable blades. Scalpels are generally more manoeuvrable through the card than craft knives, and help you to cut a more accurate line. Whichever knife you use, it is imperative to change the blade regularly.

A metal ruler or straight edge will ensure a strong, straight cut, although transparent plastic rulers are acceptable and have the added advantage that you can see the drawing beneath the ruler. Use a nifty 15cm (6in) ruler to cut short lines. Generally, when cutting, place the ruler *on the drawing* so that if your blade slips away from the ruler, it will cut harmlessly into the waste card around the outside of the drawing. An experienced paper crafter will turn their card again and again, so that each cut is made at the most comfortable angle.

FOLDING

While cutting paper is relatively straightforward, folding is less so. Whatever method you use, the crucial element is never to cut through the card along the fold line, but by using pressure, *to compress the fold line*. This is done using a tool. Whether the tool is purpose-made or improvised is a matter of personal choice and habit.

Bookbinders use a range of specialist creasing tools called bone folders. They compress the card very well, although the fold line is usually 1–2mm (⅓₂–¹⁄₁₆ in) or so away from the edge of the ruler, so if your tolerances are small, a bone folder may be considered inaccurate.

A good improvised tool is a dry ballpoint pen. The ball makes an excellent crease line, although, like the bone folder, it may be a little distance from the edge of the ruler. I have also seen people use a scissor point, an eating knife, a tool usually used for smoothing down wet clay, a fingernail and a nail file. My own preference is a dull scalpel blade (or a dull craft-knife blade). The trick is to *turn the blade upside down* (above right). It compresses the card along a reliably consistent line, immediately adjacent to the edge of the ruler.

XYZ plane axis geometry

We describe the space in which we live as 'three-dimensional' because it has three dimensions. Each dimension (axis) is assigned a letter: X, Y or Z. Note that each direction is perpendicular to the others.

This system to describe three-dimensional space is known as the Cartesian coordinate system. The point where the three axes intersect is the point of origin. The system is useful because any point in space can be plotted on the three axes and given a three-point numerical reference – negative or positive – such as (4,2,-6), in relation to the point of origin. From this, many geometric forms and surfaces can be described, including curves.

The three dimensions are:

Breadth (or width)   X axis

Depth   Y axis

Height   Z axis

The letters were so assigned because X represents a one-dimensional line drawn on the ground from left to right, across your body. The Y direction is drawn on the ground in front of you and moves towards the horizon directly in front, perpendicular to the X direction. When the X and Y directions are combined, they create a flat plane on the ground. This XY plane is horizontal, similar to laying a piece of paper on the ground. Thus, the third axis (Z) would have to be vertical, as though stacking many sheets of paper on top of one another, to create a three-dimensional block of paper. In this way, X, then XY, then XYZ create one, two and three dimensions.

It must be noted that while the above pairings of directions and letters are in common use, the X, Y and Z letters are sometimes assigned randomly to other directions.

A

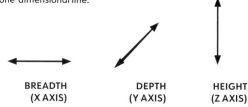

Each axis by itself is a hypothetical one-dimensional line.

B

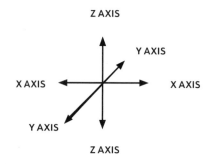

Here the XYZ axes are combined into a single three-dimensional figure.

C

Two axes combine to create flat, two-dimensional planes. Since there are three possible pairings of X, Y and Z – namely XY, XZ and YZ – there are three such planes, as shown here.

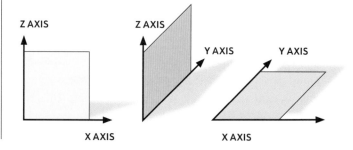

D

Three axes combine to create a three-dimensional volumetric solid, or three intersecting two-dimensional planes. The two examples look very different – one is a cube, the other an assemblage of flat planes – but they are merely different visualizations of the same planar intersections. Many other visualizations are also possible using the same three squares.

Whichever way the two examples in this illustration are rotated, they will always look the same (although the coloration may change). This means that they are fully symmetrical along the XYZ axes. Whatever is happening along one axis happens in the same way along the other two, and the structures along the three axes are identical and interchangeable. This means that the structures have three-dimensional symmetry.

Chapter by chapter, this book will explore the possibilities of rotational, two-dimensional and three-dimensional symmetry. It is a rich and fascinating journey, a wild ride for those who explore it in depth.

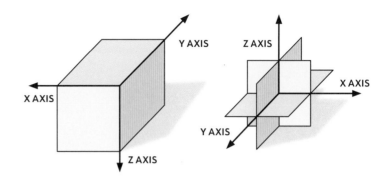

All the illustrations on this page are drawn in a flattened perspective.

E

First of all, however, a note of caution. Just because a three-dimensional structure exists in three-dimensional space, it does not necessarily exhibit three-dimensional symmetry or, indeed, symmetry of any type.

To make the point, here are a few arrangements of the three squares in the XYZ axes, chosen semi-randomly from a near-infinite number of possibilities. To a designer, each configuration will have its points of interest, but collectively, none of them exhibits the complex three-dimensional symmetry seen in the illustration above – although a few come close.

Three-dimensional symmetry is a rare and specific phenomenon, control of which will give the designer control over what is being designed.

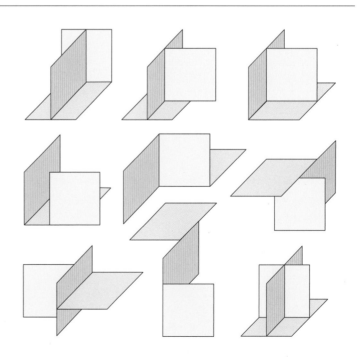

1

Thinking Flat, Thinking in 3-D

Introduction

As with all narratives, this first chapter must introduce the main characters of our story. They are faces, edges and vertices (corners). The singular of vertices is vertex.

After the introductions, the chapter shows how the three-dimensional figures they combine to make can be bisected into equal parts. This slicing up of solids introduces different notions of 2-D and 3-D symmetry, sometimes easy to understand, but perhaps sometimes a little puzzling, at least at first. Of course, it is the examples you find the most puzzling that you should focus on making, because it is from those that you will learn the most.

The chapter assumes no knowledge of geometry, no skill to cut and fold card, and, crucially, no experience of thinking and working in the third dimension. Indeed, the purpose of the book is to teach you how to do this. The key tip, though, is to make the structures with great care, looking at the drawings carefully to check that you have copied and constructed them accurately. As the saying goes, 'Measure twice, cut once.' If cutting and folding card is unfamiliar to you, take your time and enjoy the process. There is something hugely rewarding about making structures that hold together using only the most basic, inexpensive geometry equipment, and you will soon be showing off your work with pride. Making things by hand is cool.

Some of the projects may look simple or too basic, and you may think they can be overlooked. However, in truth, it is these basic structures from which the most can be learned, even for those readers with some experience of the topic. It is always best to begin a narrative at the beginning.

1.1
Thinking with Faces, Edges and Vertices

All three-dimensional objects made from flat planes have three elements: faces, edges and vertices.

Although inseparable, they each have their own independent geometries that can be studied separately. The simplest 3-D example to explore for its symmetry is a cube. This is because its faces and edges lie parallel to the Cartesian coordinates, so the relationships between the different faces and edges are easy to describe and to understand, being at 90° to each other.

A cube has six faces, twelve edges and eight vertices. The different numbers of each and thus the different three-dimensional relationships between the six faces, the twelve edges and the eight vertices mean there will be abundant patterns of symmetry to explore. It is important to understand that whatever the solid, a face is a *plane*, an edge is a *line* and a vertex is a *point*. The three are fundamentally different one from another. Knowing how to use these systems effectively is an important part of thinking and designing in the third dimension.

Here, then, are three examples that use the simple motif of squares on a cube, but relating the squares each time to face symmetry, edge symmetry and vertex symmetry.

1.1.1
Faces

A cube has six square faces. When a square is printed on each face, each square will be a flat plane. Note that there are two faces on the XY plane, two on the XZ plane and two on the YZ plane. Thus, face symmetry will be built around the three-dimensional relationships between flat planes that align to the XYZ axes.

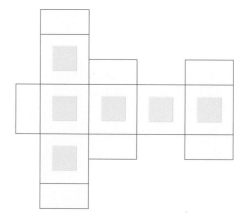

FIG. 1_1

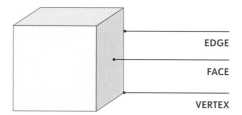

EDGE

FACE

VERTEX

1.1.2
Edges

A cube has twelve edges. When a square is printed across each edge, the square will be folded in the middle and occupy part of two adjacent faces. Note that there are four edges in each of the XYZ directions. This means that edge symmetry will be built around the three-dimensional relationships between at least two adjacent flat planes.

1.1.3
Vertices

A cube has eight vertices. When a square is printed around each vertex, it will occupy part of the three adjacent faces that meet at the vertex. This means that a quarter of the printed square will disappear from sight.

Note that a vertex is a point in the Cartesian coordinate system. It does not occupy a plane (like a face) or describe a line (like an edge).

Thus, each vertex occupies a definable point, but the relationship of one vertex to another is described only by creating an edge or a plane. Thus, vertex symmetry will be built around the three-dimensional relationships between the faces that meet at a vertex (a minimum of three) and the edges that meet at that vertex (also a minimum of three).

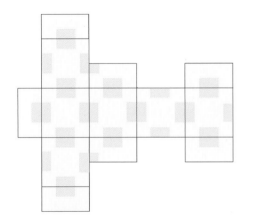

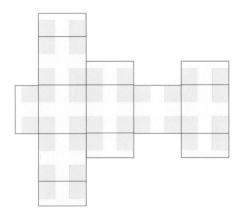

FIG. 1_2

FIG. 1_3

1.2
Bisecting a Cube with Two-dimensional Cuts

To *bisect* means to divide something into two equal halves. It can be a line, angle, plane or solid. We are working in three-dimensional space with three-dimensional figures, so we will confine ourselves to investigating how a cube can be bisected.

A cube is not the simplest solid in three-dimensional geometry, in terms of numbers. That honour goes to the tetrahedron, with just four identical faces (they are equilateral triangles, not squares), six edges and four vertices. However – as has been noted above – the cube is preferable to investigate because its XYZ axes are all at 90° to each other, so its structure and symmetry are much easier to visualize.

This section will investigate the different ways in which a cube can be bisected with one straight cut, using the different symmetries created by the faces, edges and vertices.

1.2.1
Face to opposite face

This is the first of the face, edge and vertex symmetries described in 1.1.

1.2.1.1
Elastic band

An elastic band is an excellent way to quickly investigate ways of dividing a solid into a number of identical units. It can be stretched this way and that to discover all manner of obscure and interesting possibilities, not just with one band, but with two or more.

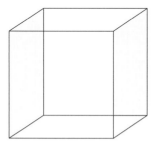

A
Select a pair of opposite faces, here shown in yellow. There are three possible pairs. Note that the faces will be parallel to each other.

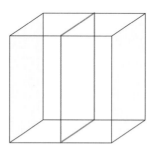

B
Imagine a continuous line around the cube (shown in green) that keeps an equal distance from the chosen faces. Such a line, being equidistant from a pair of parallel and opposite faces, will always divide the cube into two equal halves. The green line bisects the cube.

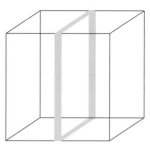

C
Using this line as a guide, an elastic band – real or imaginary – can be wrapped around the cube. When the position of the band is understood, the operations described opposite can be performed on the cube.

1.2.1.2
Separation of the halves

When the halves to each side of the elastic band are separated, the result is two simple cuboids. This is surely the simplest way to bisect a cube and, in truth, not too fascinating. But we are still at the start of our journey.

1.2.1.3
Solids

The nets for the two halves are identical. (A net is the shape a solid makes when it is cut open and flattened.) Made carefully, the solids will remain firmly locked tight without the need to use glue. The numbers refer to relative edge lengths. When making it, take careful note which of the internal edges are to be folded and which are to be cut.

These simplest of building blocks offer the chance of an early challenge. Is it possible to relate just two blocks together to create a form that is symmetrical along each of the XYZ axes, or are three blocks the minimum number, one for each axis?

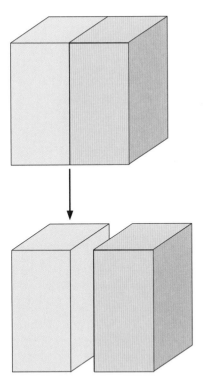

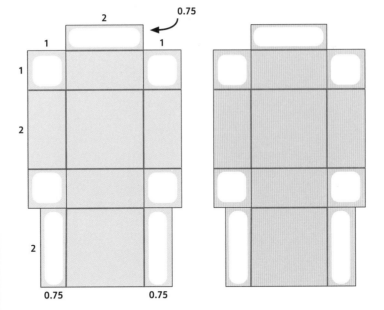

FIG. 1_4

1.2.1.4
Interlocking units

Make the units as shown. Although the illustration suggests using glue, when both units are made and fully interlocked, each will lock the other tightly shut and there is no need for glue. It's an unexpectedly stable structure, but only when assembled.

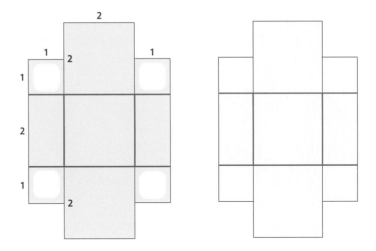

Lock the units together by aligning the square face on one unit with a half-square face on another and sliding the squares under the half squares on all four sides. When the sliding is done, a loose and raggedy structure becomes suddenly solid, stable and tidy. The transformation is very satisfying.

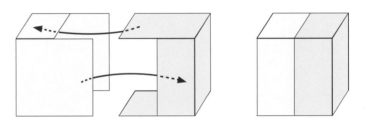

FIG. 1_5

1.2.2
Edge to opposite edge

This is the second of the face, edge and vertex symmetries described in 1.1.

1.2.2.1
Elastic band

A

Choose a pair of parallel edges that are as far apart as possible, here shown in purple. There are six such parallel pairs.

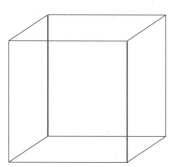

B

Imagine a continuous line (the green line) around the cube that is always equidistant from the chosen edges. Such a line will always divide the cube into two equal halves.

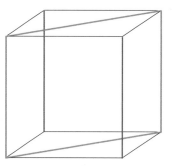

C

Using this line as a guide, an elastic band – real or imaginary – can be wrapped around the cube. When the position of the band is understood, the operations described below can be performed on the cube.

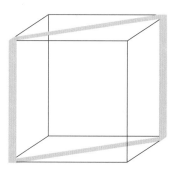

1.2.2.2
Separation of the halves

When the halves are separated, the result is two right-angled triangular prisms. Interestingly, the edges of the rectangular face are in the proportion 1:√2. This proportion can commonly be found around the world (except in the USA) in the proportion of A4 paper, or other A-sized papers or card. If the shorter side is 1 unit long, the longer side is √2 units, or 1.414... units long.

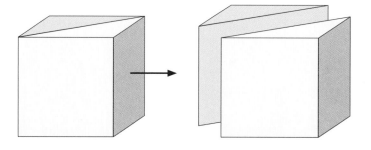

1.2.2.3
Solids

The nets (flattened-out shapes) for the two halves are identical. Made carefully, the solids will remain firmly locked without the need for glue. The numbers refer to relative edge lengths.

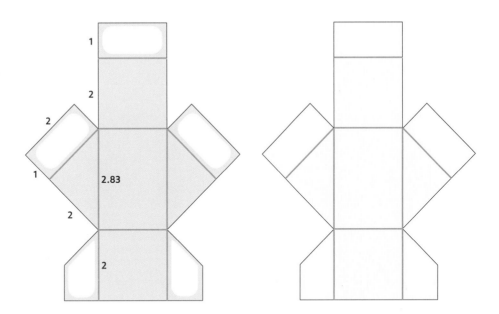

FIG. 1_6

1.2.2.4
Interlocking units

A

Make the units as shown. Although the illustration suggests using glue, when both units are made and fully interlocked, each will lock the other tightly shut and there is no need for glue. Note that the long edges are half-tabbed. It is possible to have just one long tab, but by some quirk of geometry, to do so will mean that the two units will not be identical. The advantage of half-tabbing a long edge is that it adds a knitting point in the middle of the long edge, thus strengthening the connection between the two units.

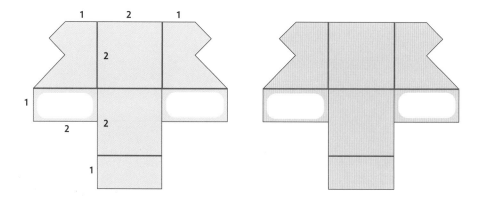

B

Lock the units together by aligning the protruding tabs on one unit with the diagonal edge on the other, along both the top and the bottom faces of the units. Slide the units together so that all four tabs disappear inside, to leave a clean diagonal edge where the colours meet. A stronger lock can be made by making all the tabs dovetailed so that when interlocked, they hook around each other.

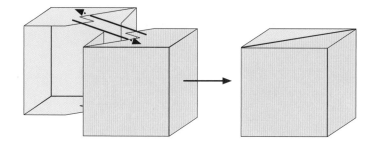

FIG. 1_7

1.2.3
Vertex to opposite vertex

This is the third of the face, edge and vertex symmetries described in 1.1.

1.2.3.1
Elastic band

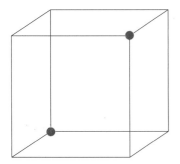

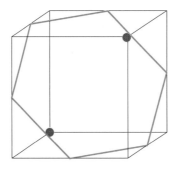

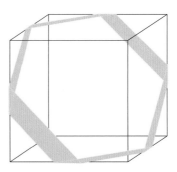

A

Choose a pair of vertices as far apart as possible. As before, be sure that you have chosen a correct pairing.

B

The continuous green line is always at the mid-point between the two chosen vertices. The vertices of the line are at the mid-points of six edges and, surprisingly, describe a regular hexagon. The relationship between a cube (three-dimensional, square faces and 90° angles) and a hexagon (two-dimensional, six-sided faces and angles of 120°) may seem unlikely, but this simple construction clearly reveals it. It's a fascinating and beautiful piece of geometry.

C

Using this green line as a guide, an elastic band – real or imaginary – can be wrapped around the cube. When the position of the band is understood, the operations described opposite can be performed on the cube.

1.2.3.2
Separation of the halves

When the halves are separated, a regular hexagon is revealed along the line of the cut. Perhaps surprisingly, other than the hexagon, the other angles are all 90° and 45°. It seems as though two systems of geometry – square (orthogonal) geometry and triangular/hexagonal (isometric) geometry – have been mysteriously mixed.

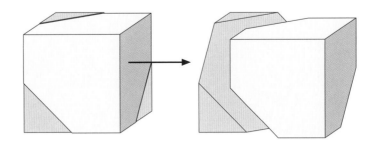

1.2.3.3
Solids

This is a relatively complex construction, made easier because there are only three different angles of note and three different lengths. The compensation is that it is also one of the most surprising and beautiful bisections that can be made, not just with a cube, but with any solid.

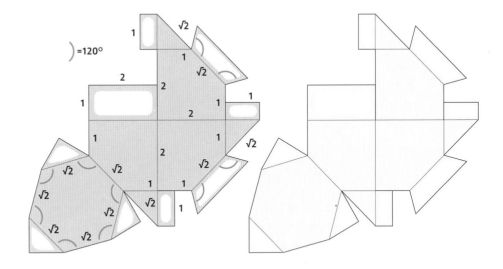

FIG. 1_8

1.2.3.4
Interlocking units

A

The units are easier to make than the solid version because there is no need to create a solid hexagonal plane. Indeed, it is difficult to see the hexagonal plane in the final construction amid the many 45° edges and square tabs.

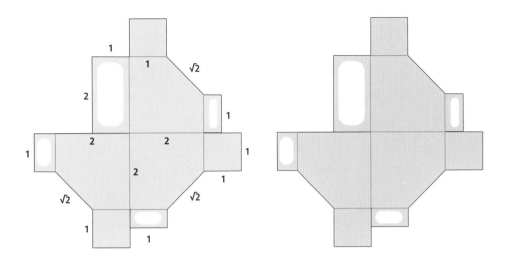

B

The square tabs on one unit are placed opposite the 45° edges on the other and then slid underneath the edges to lock the units together. Each tab on a unit is in one of the three Cartesian planes (XY, XZ and YZ). This means that the lock is fully three-dimensional, which in turn means that once interlocked, the units stay together strongly. This is because in whichever direction the units are separated, there is a tab to oppose the separation and keep the units together. It's an unexpected and very satisfying example of three-dimensional geometry.

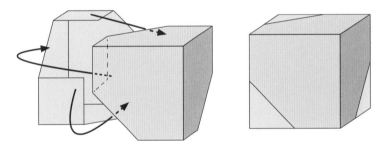

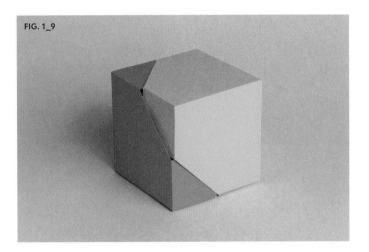

FIG. 1_9

1.3
Bisecting a Cube with Three-dimensional Cuts

In the previous section, we saw how a cube can be divided into two equal halves using a simple, straight, two-dimensional cut, as though the cube were made of wood and were being cut into two pieces by a saw blade.

This section will show how it is also possible to bisect a cube using a more complex three-dimensional cut, impossible to make with a saw blade. Not only do these cuts create a more complex surface on the outside of the cube, but also the cuts are more complex on the inside, dividing the interior into a series of facets around the centre point.

This complexity is the result of bisecting the cube three-dimensionally. However, we are still bisecting the cube along only one of the XYZ axes, instead of along all three axes, so although the results are complex, the symmetry is not yet truly three-dimensional.

1.3.1
Face to opposite face

In this first example, the shapes of the two identical units are built around opposing faces.

1.3.1.1
Graphic separation

A

These are the two faces, marked in yellow.

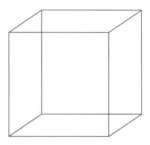

B

An intricate path (in green) can be traced around eight of the twelve edges of the cube so that each of the yellow faces is at the symmetrical centre of the bisection.

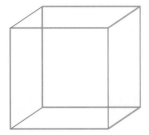

C

The path cuts the surface of the cube into two identical halves, each consisting of three square faces. Notice how the two yellow faces in A (left) are the middle squares of the three that create each unit. We can now re-form the cube either as two intermeshing solid halves, or as two interlocking surfaces.

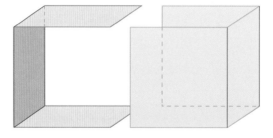

1.3.1.2
Solids

A

Each unit consists of three square faces. We can make a solid equal to half the volume of the cube by creating edges that connect each vertex with the centre point of the cube.

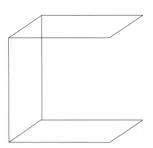

B

We can find the centre point of the cube by creating a large X, as shown. The blue dot indicates the centre.

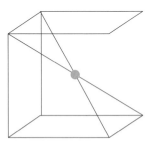

C

Now, connect the remaining four vertices also to the centre point.

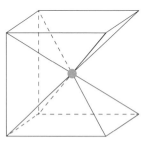

D

The 3-D unit consists of three four-sided pyramids. The base of each pyramid is a square face of the cube. This complex but beautiful structure is half the volume of the cube.

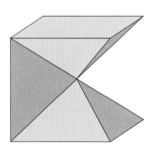

E

If you know a little of the Pythagoras theorem, you can perhaps use it to deduce the relative lengths of the sides of the eight triangles. All the triangles are the same shape and size. Another way to construct the triangles is to construct the angles, given here (approximate to two decimal places).

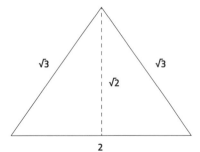

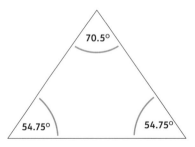

F

A third way to construct the triangles is simply to use A4 paper (or perhaps A5 or A6). Drawing the two diagonals across the sheet will automatically create the triangles. Draw the diagonals, then use a ruler and knife to cut out the coloured triangles.

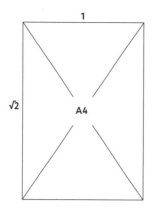
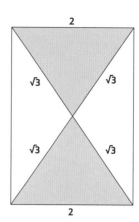

G

Here are the two identical nets. It is not easy to draw them accurately by hand, so the preferred method is to use graphic software.

Note that some of the glue tabs are shaped like the roof of a house. Those tabs attached to a square have angles of 54.75° at the base of the 'roof', whereas those attached to triangles have angles of 70.5° at the vertex adjacent to the apex of the triangle and 54.75° at the other end of the 'roof'.

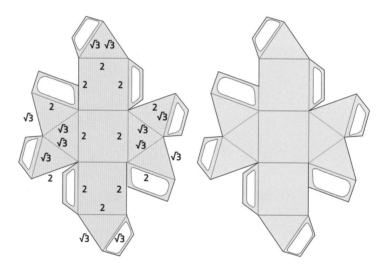

H

Made carefully, the two halves will lock together to create a simple-looking cube that conceals the intricacies of its beautiful internal structure. The units will also sit loosely together square-to-square, offering many possibilities for multifaceted structures. Making eight or more of these units will offer many exciting opportunities to assemble complex and intriguing hyperstructures.

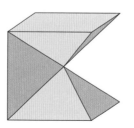
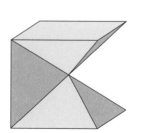
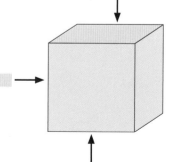

FIG. 1_10

1.3.1.3
Interlocking units

In contrast to the solid units, the interlocking surface units are very simple to construct and make. However, peculiarly, the units cannot be made identically. Note that while the three square faces are placed in the same three-in-a-row vertical position in both units, where one unit has a tab, the other unit has a 'no tab' space. That's definitely strange...but why does it happen?

The two units will lock together very solidly. One reason for the solidity is that the tabs are positioned in each of the XYZ directions, so the cube is held together three-dimensionally. Another reason is that the cube has eight chunky tabs that create a lot of friction to hold them tightly in place.

FIG. 1_11

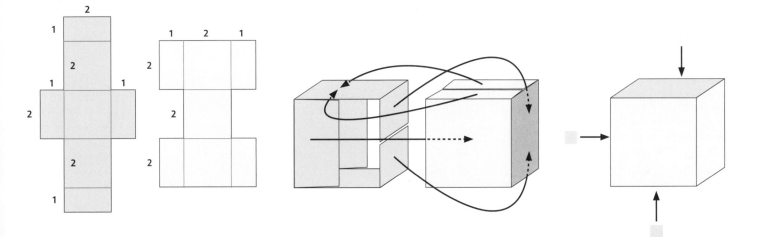

1.3.2
Edge to opposite edge

This construction is an interesting anomaly, the exception that proves the rule. Essentially, it is impossible to create a *unique* unit that uses a pair of opposing edges around which two identical units can be built. Here are the reasons.

A

Here are two opposing edges on a cube. The task is to design two identical units around them.

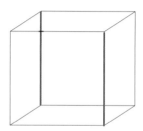

B

Since our starting point is an edge, we must incorporate the face to each side of each edge into the unit. The edge on each unit thus becomes a fold between two square faces. However, we have not incorporated a third face on each unit to create the required number of six faces on a solid cube. So the question is, how can we add these extra two faces, or indeed, *can* they be added?

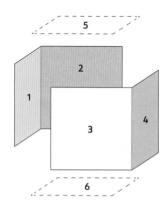

C

There are two possible ways to add a third face to each unit. The top line shows how a third face can be added to the front of the unit. However, this creates the same arrangement of three squares made in the previous section (1.3.1). The centre of the unit is now a face, not an edge. This means the edge shown by a thick line is no longer the centre of the unit. This three-square solution is not unique.

The second possibility is to add the third face to the top of the unit. However, this creates the same arrangement of three squares seen in the next section (1.3.3). The centre of the unit is no longer an edge, but a corner, here shown as a purple dot. So this second possibility also doesn't create a unique solution.

From this, it can be seen that adding a third square face to each unit does not give a unique result. But what if the face is split into triangles?

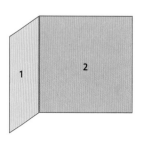
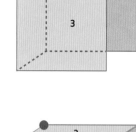
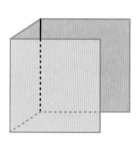
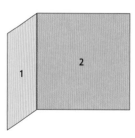
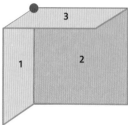
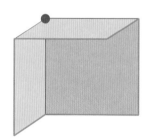

D

This time, the third face is split into two triangles, here coloured blue. Each triangle is half a square and each spans the gap between the edges of square 1 and square 2.

This seems to be the result we need. The two wedge-shaped units connect when the rectangular faces – here seen with green edges – touch. The meeting of the two wedges satisfies the criterion of being equidistant from the opposite edges.

So have we found an answer? Well, no. We have seen this unit earlier, in 1.2.2. It is not a unique solution.

This means that the three solutions we have found all belong more uniquely to other systems of dividing the cube into two halves. There is no unique solution to the problem of creating two identical units with a three-dimensional cut, with opposite edges placed centrally on an edge unit. How unexpected and fascinating is that?

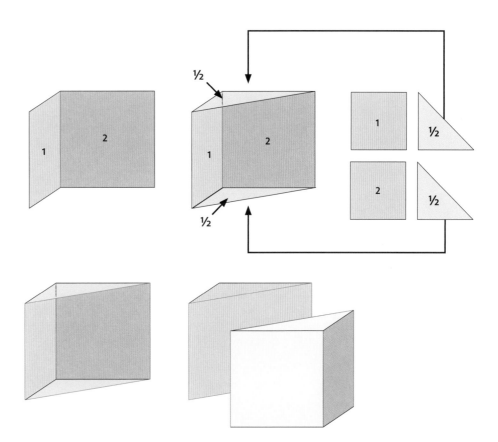

1.3.3
Vertex to opposite vertex

In this final example, the shapes of the two identical units are built around opposing vertices.

1.3.3.1
Graphic separation

A

Two opposite vertices are selected on the cube, here marked with purple dots. Be sure to choose a pair that really are as far apart as possible.

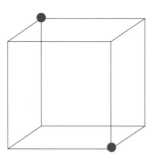

B

A path can be traced along six edges of the cube so that each marked vertex is at the meeting point of three square faces and the path is midway between those vertices.

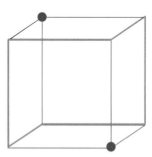

C

When the path is cut open, the cube separates into two identical halves. Each half has square faces in each of the XYZ directions.

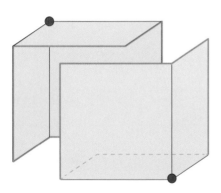

D

Extend edges from each of the six vertices to the centre point of the cube, here marked with a green dot. The triangles created are the same as those seen in 1.3.1.2E above. Note that this creates three pyramids, the square bases of which are faces of the cube. Compare this arrangement of pyramids with those in 1.3.1.2C.

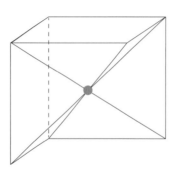

E

The three pyramids are here rendered as one solid unit.

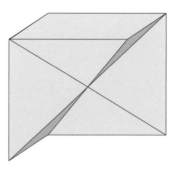

1.3.3.2
Solids

A

The method of constructing the solids is identical to the method for constructing the unit made in 1.3.1.2E–G. Refer to pp. 29–30 for tips.

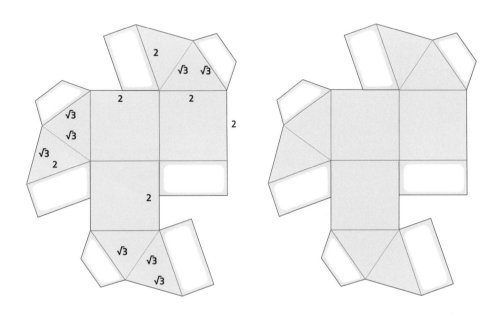

B

As in 1.3.1, the plainness of the exterior hides an unexpectedly complex internal structure. Make a number of the units and experiment with ways to interlock them in XYZ directions, triangle face to triangle face, or square to square.

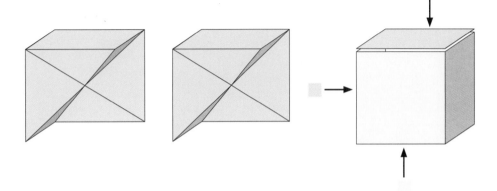

FIG. 1_12

1.3.3.3
Interlocking units

A

The modules are pleasingly simple to make, but, unlike their cousins seen in 1.3.1.3, the tabs on the two units are placed in identical positions. However, it is important to note that each unit is the *mirror image* of the other.

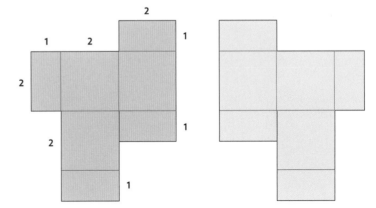

B

There are many ways to interlock the eight tabs into the cube, one by one, but only one sequence will be quick and easy. Can you find it? When complete, the cube will lock together very strongly.

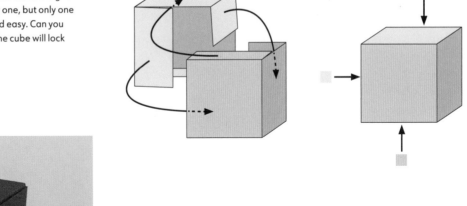

FIG. 1_13

Rotational Symmetry

Introduction

Rotational symmetry is the simplest and most versatile of the four symmetry operations (rotation, reflection, translation and glide reflection). This chapter shows how it can be used two-dimensionally and then revised to work in three dimensions.

Two-dimensional rotational symmetry is easy to understand, but assembling folded units using three-dimensional rotational symmetry can be an absorbing puzzle, the principles of which must be well understood if success is to be achieved. This chapter will ease you carefully from two dimensions to three.

The key to understanding the principles is to understand a multi-unit structure similar to the iris encircling a camera lens, in which each unit overlaps the next around a centre point, until the final unit overlaps the first. This creates a continuous rotation of units, without a beginning or an end. The number of units and their relation to one another, including any folds, dictates how the symmetry will play out to create a two-dimensional surface or a three-dimensional form.

As the chapter progresses, examples of increasing sophistication are presented for you to make, and questions are asked to check that you understand the logic of what you are making. After all, the purpose of this book is to teach the principles of thinking and designing in the third dimension. Simply to assemble the units without understanding the basic principles of rotational symmetry would perhaps leave you with a fascinating object in the hand, but without any newly learned knowledge. So, as you work through the pages, you are strongly encouraged to analyse what you are making, to study everything with patience and care, and to understand how one exercise relates to another.

2.1
Thinking Flat

Before moving on to consider rotational symmetry in the third dimension, it is helpful first to consider it in two dimensions. The two circular fans shown here look similar, but are made in very different ways.

2.1.1
Circular fan from a circle

A

Cut a circle at least 20cm (8in) in diameter. From the centre point, use a protractor to divide the 360° into sixteen angles, each of 22.5°. If you are familiar with origami, you may know an alternative method, folding the circle into 180, then 90, then 45, then 22.5°. Whichever method you choose, all the folds must be valleys (see p. 6).

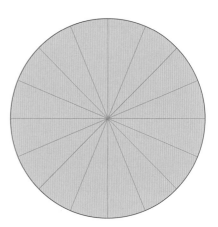

B

This is the pattern so far. Double-check that all your folds are valleys. Turn the paper over...

C

...so that all the folds are now mountains.

D

Squeeze a mountain fold and place it on the adjacent mountain, creating a valley fold midway between them. This should be done by holding the paper in the air, not by folding on a table. Alternatively, use a protractor and measure an angle of 11.25° to locate the position of the valley between the mountains.

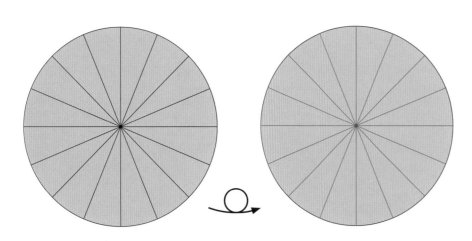

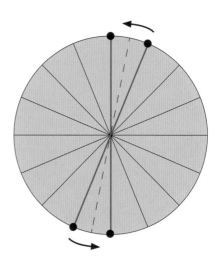

E

This is the result.

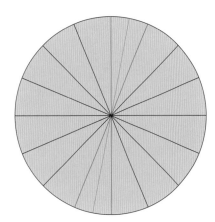

F

Using your preferred method of folding, continue to make valley folds between the mountains. Be careful to do this with extreme accuracy.

G

This step will test your accuracy. Gather up all the mountains and valleys, except for an unfolded (flattened) valley fold down the centre at the front and the same at the back. Organize the layers so that there are eight double layers to the left and to the right of the centre line. Press everything flat, strengthening all the folds.

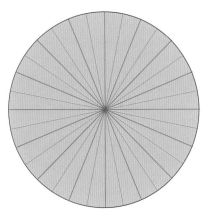

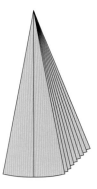

H

Using scissors, cut off about 4mm (roughly ⅛in) on a 20cm (8in) diameter circle, or proportionately more or less, depending on the size of your circle. If in doubt, cut off less than you think you need to remove, proceed to the end of the step sequence, then, if the fan will not open flat, refold to this step and cut off a little more.

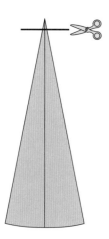

I

Open all the layers, remembering also to fold the flattened valleys at the front and back.

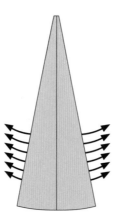

J

With a little encouragement, the fan will lie flat. If it will not, stretch the pleats away from the centre point, to increase the diameter. If it still will not lie flat, return to step H and snip off a little more paper...but not much.

The result will be a beautiful fan, with no hole at the centre point. It is a near-perfect visualization of two-dimensional rotational symmetry. Without the snip in step H, the fan will forever remain a three-dimensional cone.

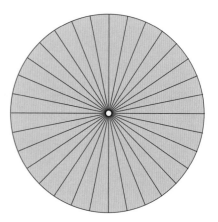

FIG. 2_1

2.1.2
Circular fan from a strip

A

The key to making this design successfully
is to know the proportion of the short side
of the paper to the long side. The short
side of the paper relates to the radius of
a circle, and the long side to the circumference
of the same circle.

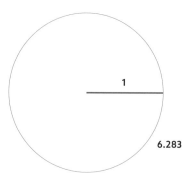

B

This is the supposedly correct proportion of
the paper. However, in reality, 6.283:1 is a little
short to make a circular fan...

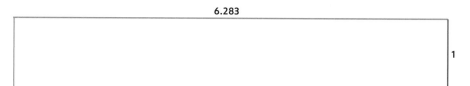

C

...so the length should be increased to
seven times the short side. Thus, the correct
proportion is 7:1.

D

Use a strip of paper about 1m (3ft) long. Divide the length into ten equal sections, using only valley folds. It may be helpful to prepare a length of paper that can easily be measured into forty equal divisions, such as 1m (every division will be 2.5cm) or 30in (every division will be ¾in).

E

Further divide the paper into twenty, again using only valley folds.

F

And again...further divide the paper into forty. Turn the paper over...

G

...so that all the folds are mountains.

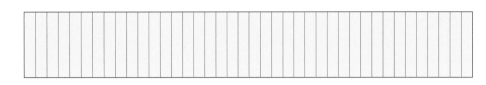

H

Using a technique similar to the one used earlier in 2.1.1D, create valley folds exactly midway between all the mountain folds. This will divide the paper into a long accordion with eighty parts.

I

Cut off just one division of the eighty.

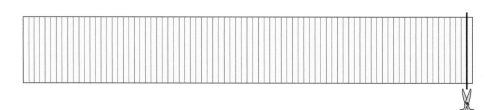

J

Add glue to a single division at one end.

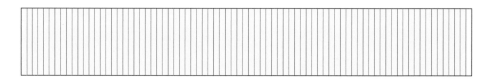

K

Curl the pleated strip into a cylinder and very carefully overlap the final division at one end with the glued division at the other end. The resulting cookie-cutter cylinder will have seventy-eight divisions. It is advisable to practise the gluing and joining together before committing to both, so that you are familiar with what to do and the joint is perfect and invisible. Make sure the glued and overlapped section is as flexible as all the other folds, and not stiff in any way.

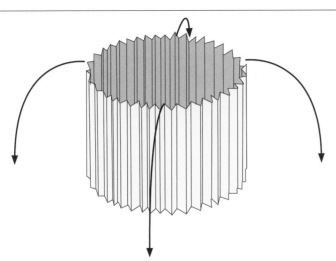

L

Strengthen all the folds. Then splay the top edge outwards to become the perimeter of the fan, while simultaneously bunching the bottom edge tightly together to become the densely packed centre point of the fan. This can take a little while, so be patient and persevere. If the folds become ill-defined, take time to strengthen them again. Eventually, the fan will lie flat and will not spring into three dimensions.

M

To ensure the fan remains flat, cut a circle of stiff card, including a hole in the middle. The circle should be a little smaller than the fan. Add glue liberally to one surface and place it behind the fan. Help the fan to adhere to the support by placing a book or similar weight on the fan.

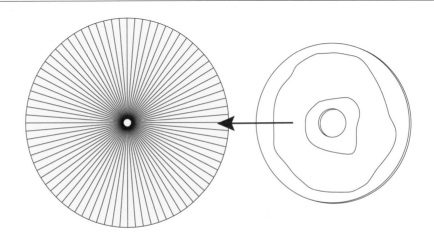

N

This is the result. The supporting card (shown by the ring of dots) is to the rear. Turn it over.

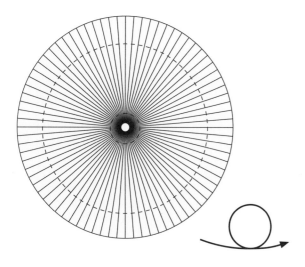

O

This is the reverse side. Turn it back to the front.

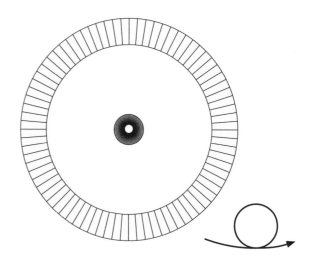

P

The fan is simple in concept, but it must be made perfectly if it is to look good. When made well and to the correct proportion, the perimeter will be an almost flat, straight edge that does not zigzag up and down. By contrast, at the centre, the edge of the tightly folded paper will stand vertically. The form is one of the most perfect and beautiful that can be made by folding paper. Now make one with a diameter of 2m (6ft 6in)! The seventy-eight divisions are not an optimal number, just a suggestion. With larger sizes, the number can be increased to 100 and more. However, whatever the number of divisions, the paper should always be proportioned 7:1.

Although it is an example of two-dimensional rotational symmetry, it is the folded structure of this circular fan that will help us to understand and create the three-dimensional rotational symmetry structures that follow.

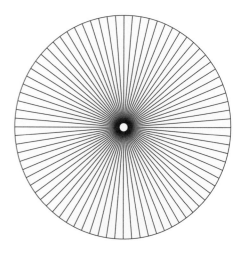

FIG. 2_2

2.2
Moving from 2-D to 3-D

The circular fans made in the previous section were an excellent way to experience and understand how examples of two-dimensional rotational symmetry can be created. This section eases us from thinking flat to thinking in three dimensions. It takes the principles by which the fans were made and adapts them into the third dimension.

2.2.1
Deconstructing and reinterpreting the circular fans

The fans were a succession of folds, alternating mountain-valley-mountain-valley and so on. They could be deconstructed and made from many separate pieces of paper or card with a valley fold in the middle, as shown here.

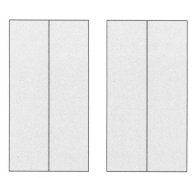

A
When folded and placed side by side, two pieces look like this.

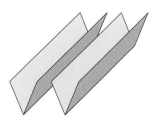

B
The two edges marked in red can be brought together...

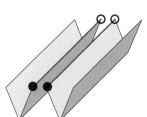

C
...to create a form resembling the letter W, with a mountain fold in the middle.

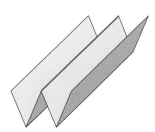

D

Any number of similar units can be joined in the same way to create a zigzag surface of any length. This is how the fans were made, but using only one piece.

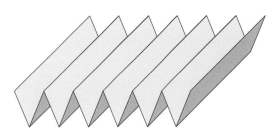

E

However, there is another way in which the same units can be joined edge to edge. Here, the *short* edges marked in red are joined.

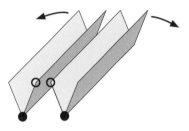

F

Note how the two red edges have united to create one edge, allowing the two units to splay apart.

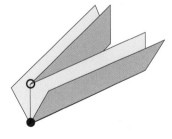

G

Here, six units are being joined. Note how like colours unite to create a folded edge, and how the edge on the extreme left connects to the edge on the extreme right, to close the circle.

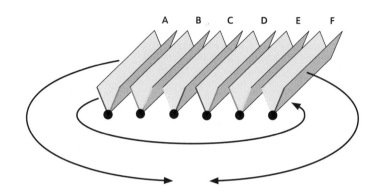

H

The six units will spread out to create a near-flat snowflake. However, the six-unit assembly will probably prefer not to remain flat, but to bunch together to elevate the centre point to a standing position, somewhat like a six-sided pyramid. The number of units is discretionary.

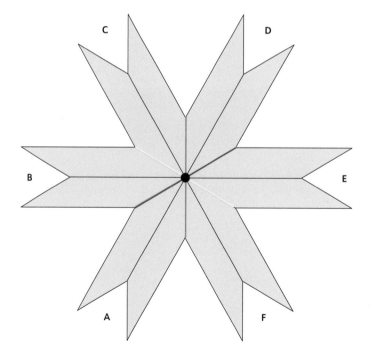

I

It is possible to join the raw edges as described in step G (opposite) using tape, as shown in the photograph below (the pieces of tape are the off-white squares). However, the result is rough-looking and unattractive.

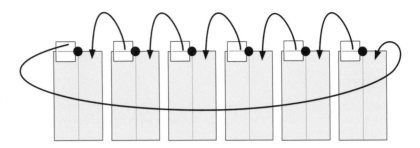

FIG. 2_3

J

A better solution is to add a connecting tab to one of the two raw edges that are joined, so that the fold between the tab and the unit becomes the line of the joint. The result is a stable, attractive form.

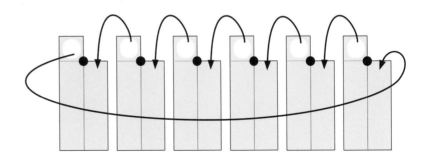

2.2.2
Constructing a vertex

Instead of joining a large number of units to create a fan-like or pyramidic structure, joining just three in the same way will create a vertex. Note the addition of glue tabs, which will secure each unit to the next around the vertex without the need to use tape...

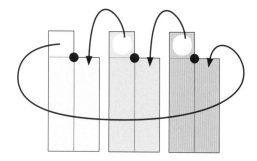

...like this (right). We can now use this principle to create a large number of three-dimensional forms.

However, there are two problems. First, the tabs are visible and should be hidden. Second, we need to add tabs at the other ends of all the units so that more than one vertex can be created. In this way, each unit will become an edge of a polyhedron, connecting two vertices.

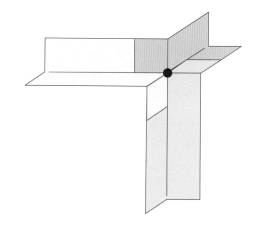

FIG. 2_4

A

These are the amended units. Note the addition of the A and B rectangles and of a second glue tab. The glue tabs are staggered.

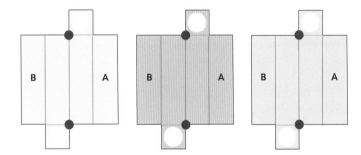

B

Glue the tabs together around the vertex, as shown. Then fold in the A flaps. When folded, they will hide the tabs. They may lock themselves in place, but if they misbehave, add a little glue to hold them down.

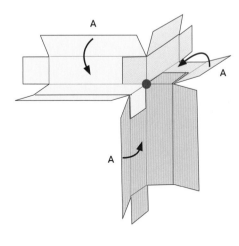

D

The B flaps may appear unnecessary. However, when other units are locked into place to create other vertices, they will be used to hide the unsightly tabs around each new vertex, in the way that the A flaps were used before. The A and B flaps also serve to strengthen the units.

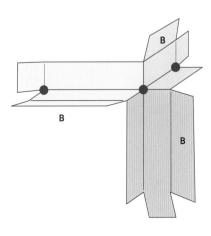

C

The vertex is now complete.

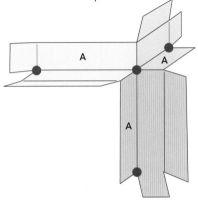

2.2.3
Making simple edge polyhedra

The simplest polyhedron to make is
a tetrahedron. It has four triangular
faces, four vertices and six edges.
Three edges meet at every vertex.

A

Each unit will create an edge of the
tetrahedron. Since there are six edges,
there will be six units.

One important component of three-
dimensional thinking is to identify and use
three-dimensional symmetry. So the question
is: can the six edges of a tetrahedron be
coloured to show symmetry? The answer is yes.

For each edge, there is an edge at the
opposite side of the solid. The two edges are
perpendicular to each other. Together, they
describe two of the three XYZ directions. There
are three such pairs (3 × 2 pairs = 6 edges).

So it is possible to colour the six edges
symmetrically, using just three colours,
as shown in step B.

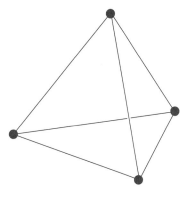

B

To make an edge tetrahedron, make six units
as shown, in three colour-pairs. Join them as
described in 2.2.2A–D, being extra careful to
put units of the same colour on opposite sides
of the solid. Before gluing the units, fit them
together loosely in order to understand the
structure. Interestingly, the assembled units
will stand on an edge, on a vertex or on a face,
allowing the tetrahedron to be displayed in
pleasing and unfamiliar orientations.

Is there a way to create a symmetrical
arrangement of coloured edges using only two
colours, or is the three-colour solution shown
here the only solution?

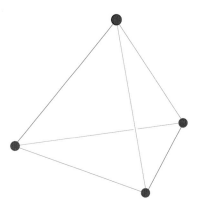

FIG. 2_5

C

A more complex example of edge-colouring symmetry to explore is a cube. It has twelve edges, so the possibilities for colouring are:

6 colours   2 units of each colour

4 colours   3 units of each colour

3 colours   4 units of each colour

2 colours   6 units of each colour

The example shown here uses three colours, with four units of each colour. Notice that the four units of each colour lie in one of the XYZ directions. Is it possible to create a symmetrical arrangement of edges using six, four or two colours?

One interesting – even annoying – feature of the edge cube is that it is very unstable. It is impossible to keep all the faces perpendicular to one another and all the vertices at exactly 90°. If the units are elongated, the cube becomes extremely unstable and can be flattened or twisted in many extraordinary ways, like a toy. The cube in the photograph may look stable, but it was posed for the shot.

FIG. 2_6

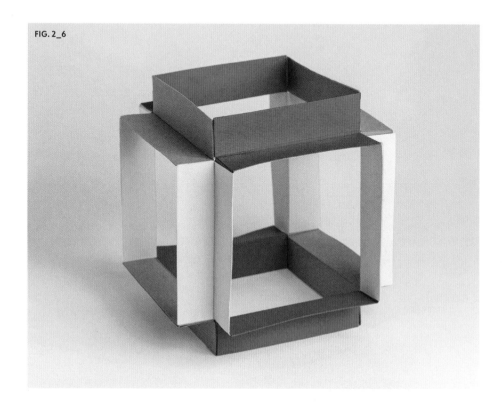

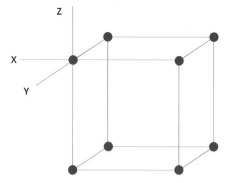

D

Like a cube, an octahedron has twelve edges, and like a tetrahedron, it has triangular faces. The novelty of its structure is that it has eight faces and that four edges meet at every vertex, not three. However, the construction of each vertex is the same as before, except that four edge units are glued together at each vertex, instead of three.

In the example of colour symmetry shown here, there are three colours and four units of each colour. The placement of four identical colours describes a square around the perimeter of the octahedron. The square planes are in each of the XYZ directions.

The octahedron is assembled from the simple units shown in 2.2.2. The units lack the aesthetic neatness of the more complex units used to make the cube (2.2.3C), but they are much quicker to make and to assemble. If the intrusion of coloured squares on to neighbouring units troubles you, simply cut out squares the same colour as the units being imposed upon and glue them over the offending invaders.

E

Each of the three squares created by four edge units with identical colours describes one of the XYZ directions and is orthogonal to the others (they intersect at 90° to each other). This exact form will be seen again in 4.4.3. Are other symmetrical colour patterns possible using six, four, three or two colours?

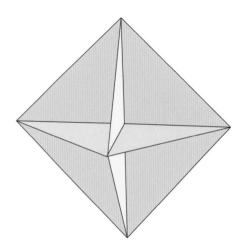

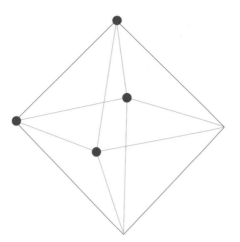

FIG. 2_7

2.2.4
The edge icosahedron

The complex icosahedron is the least regarded of the basic polyhedra, perhaps because each of its twenty faces has an odd number of edges (3), and an odd number of edges meet at each vertex (5). These asymmetric (odd) numbers would appear to create little of interest to someone studying three-dimensional symmetry. However, to think this would be a mistake.

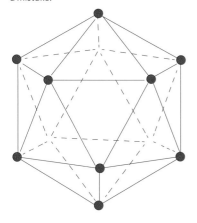

B

After marking the initial six edges with one colour, randomly choose an unmarked edge and mark it with a second colour. Using that edge as a reference, create a pattern of distribution across six edges that is identical to the first distribution across six edges. Then repeat with the third, fourth and fifth colours, each time beginning with a random unmarked edge. Take time to understand the logic of the distribution, which at first can appear arbitrary. It is not.

After understanding the distribution of coloured edges, make an icosahedron from thirty units. Note that five units will meet at each vertex.

If the coloured edges are to be distributed symmetrically, it is a very challenging structure to make. However, you will learn much about three-dimensional thinking if you persevere.

The icosahedron is assembled from the simple units shown in 2.2.2. The units lack the aesthetic neatness of the more complex units used to make the cube (2.2.3C), but they are much quicker to make and assemble.

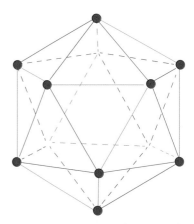

A

It is possible to colour the thirty edges symmetrically with just five colours. Each colour is used on six edges. The six edges are shown here.

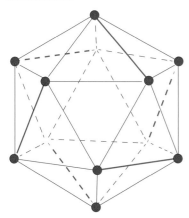

FIG. 2_8

2.2.5
Exploring the icosahedron further

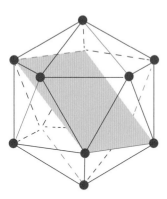

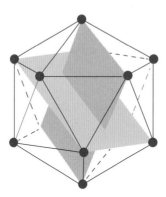

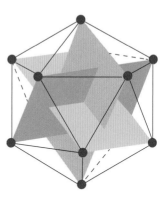

A

We can explore the icosahedron further for other beautiful examples of three-dimensional symmetry. Notice that when six edges are nominated to be the same colour, they lie in three diametrically opposed pairs. Here is the first pair of edges, connected by a pink rectangle. The rectangle bisects the icosahedron into equal halves.

B

The new rectangle connects a second pair of diametrically opposed edges. Note that it cuts through the plane of the first rectangle at 90°. That's a big surprise.

C

Finally, here is the third rectangle, connecting the final pair of diametrically opposed edges. Surprisingly, all the icosahedron's twelve vertices have been included in the arrangement of the three planes.

If you are wondering...yes, it is possible to create the same three planes for all five edge-unit colours in the same icosahedron. The result is an icosahedron with indented pyramids on all its twenty triangular faces (not shown). The complex entanglement of fifteen planes that slice through the centre point of the solid is invisible behind these dimples and need not be made.

D

This is the final form. Its relationship to an icosahedron is not immediately apparent, even to someone familiar with the solid. Fascinatingly, the orthogonal intersection of the three planes at the centre point is the same as the orthogonal intersection of the three planes for the seemingly unrelated octahedron (see 2.2.3E). This connection between the symmetries of two very different-looking polyhedra is very unexpected. The following pages explain how to make this intriguing form.

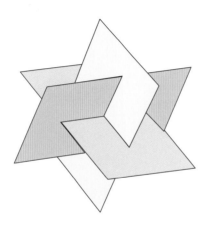

E

To make a three-planes example, we must first know the proportion of the rectangle. Predictably, it isn't a random proportion, but easily describable. This is how it is made. Begin with a pentagon.

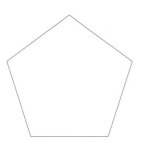

F

Draw a circle centred on a vertex and with its radius the length of an edge. The circle will connect with two vertices.

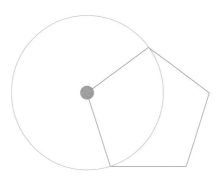

G

Drop a perpendicular from the centre of the circle to the circumference. Note that it will drop a little below the bottom edge of the pentagon.

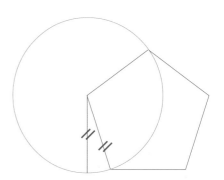

H

Draw a diagonal across the pentagon.

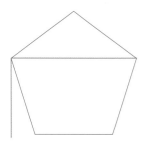

I

Complete the rectangle. The short side is the edge length of a pentagon, the long side is the diagonal of that pentagon.

J

This is the final rectangle, proportioned 1:1.618...

K

Cut out four identical rectangles, each proportioned 1:1.618. Note that two are the same colour. For the moment, put the two rectangles of the same colour to one side.

L

On the two uniquely coloured rectangles, draw the centre lines.

M

Lay the short edge of one rectangle against the longer drawn centre line of the other, lining up the two vertical centre lines as shown, and mark the corners.

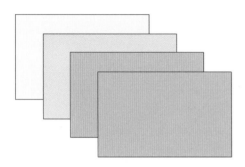

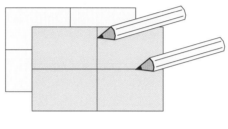

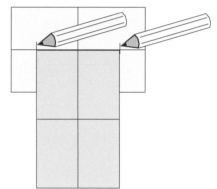

N

Repeat with the other unit, then, on both units, cut a straight line between the marks using a knife. It is advisable to cut a second and parallel line a tiny, tiny fraction away from the first, so that in the next step, one card passes easily – but not loosely – through the other because the slit has become a narrow slot...

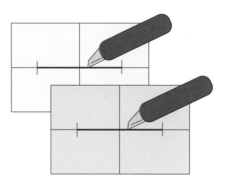

O

...like this.

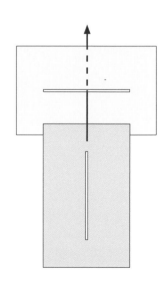

P

Draw the same centre lines on the third and fourth units, then draw the extra line, as shown. For once, its exact position is unimportant.

Q

Finally, make cuts on each of the units, as shown.

R

This is the result. As with the other units, it is advisable to widen the horizontal slits with a second, parallel cut.

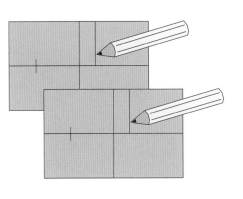

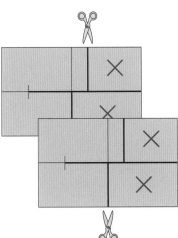

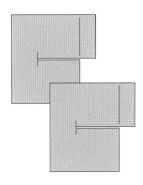

S

Turn one of the units upside down and apply glue, as shown. Push the units through the existing slots. When pushed fully through, the structure will suddenly tighten and become very stable. Before gluing the card, practise the final assembly.

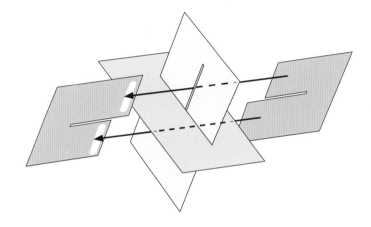

T

This is the final result. The structure is deceptively simple – just three intersecting planes – but the three-dimensional symmetry is both beautiful and complex.

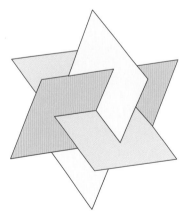

FIG. 2_9

2.3
Iris-like Rotations

Overlapping planes around a central point creates a visual effect similar to that of a camera iris. However, whereas a camera iris is two-dimensional, it is possible also to create the effect in three dimensions. We will see how both can be made.

2.3.1
Transforming a two-dimensional iris into three dimensions

Any number of flat shapes – not necessarily squares or shapes with straight edges – can be arranged to meet at one point. Here is a simple example, using eight squares.

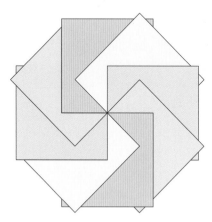

A
When reduced to four squares, each square occupies 90° of the 360° around the centre point. The arrangement is flat and symmetrical.

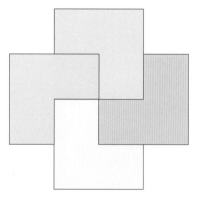

B

When one square is removed, the arrangement becomes asymmetric. Three angles of 90° do not occupy a full 360° of rotation. However, if the third square is pulled around to interlock with the first square, a symmetrical vertex of 3 × 90° angles will be created. This is how it is made.

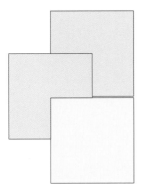

C

Take three squares and fold each down the centre line. Unfold.

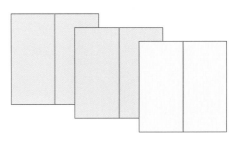

D

Glue the flat arrangement of squares together, as shown. Finally, apply glue where shown, then stick the bottom square behind the top square. Re-form the three valley folds so that the structure becomes three-dimensional...

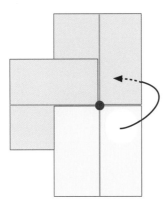

E

...like this. Note how the structure is completely symmetrical and how each unit locks behind one neighbour but in front of the neighbour on the other side. This iris has become a three-dimensional vertex.

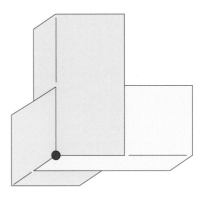

FIG. 2_10

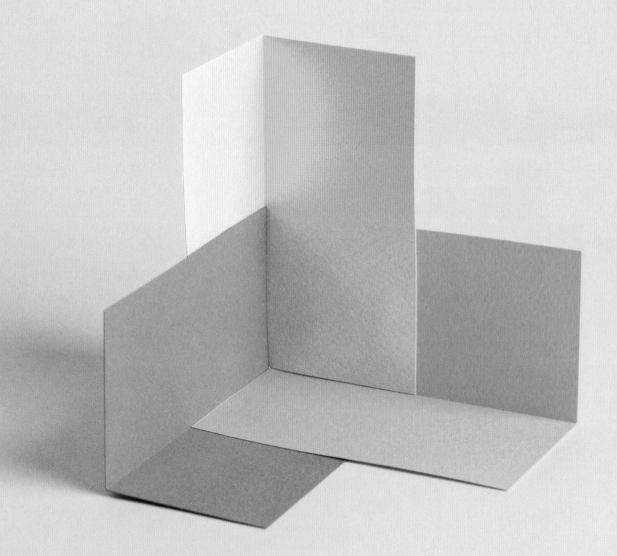

2.3.2
From a vertex to a cube

A

The vertex created in the previous section can be duplicated to create a cube with eight vertices. To understand how the units interweave in front of and behind each other to create the full cube, we must first understand that a cube can be wrapped in each of the XYZ directions, as shown here.

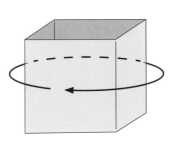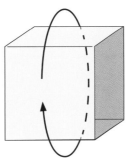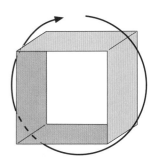

B

Each of the tubes can be cut into four units. The cuts divide each face into two equal rectangles. Each unit is a square folded down the centre.

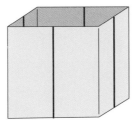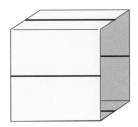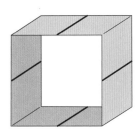

C

This is the set of twelve units. There are three colours and four units of each colour. Each unit has a valley fold down the centre.

D

The twelve units will glue together to create
a solid cube.

The assembly is a puzzle. Which part of
which unit should be behind or in front of its
neighbours? What colour should the unit be?
Why? Before gluing anything into its final
position, be sure you know it is correctly placed.
Think about how you know it is correct. Try to
understand the structure logically. Nothing is
random: everything is where it is for a reason,
and often for several reasons.

If everything is correct, each face of the cube
will be a two-colour chequerboard. Opposite
faces will have the same two colours.

The key to assembling the structure correctly is
to understand that the four units of one colour
lie in the same X, Y or Z direction, as shown in
step C on the previous page. The units in the
three directions combine to create the cube.

This simple cube is a classic three-dimensional
construction, requiring a thorough
understanding of three-dimensional symmetry
and demanding a high level of three-
dimensional thinking. It is also very satisfying
to make. Once the interlocking system is
understood, the system runs itself until the
cube is completed.

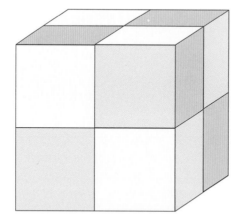

FIG. 2_11

E

The square unit, when folded, is divided into two planes, each a 2 × 1 rectangle. However, the unit can also be a different proportion, so that – for example – when folded, each plane becomes a 4 × 1 rectangle, as shown here.

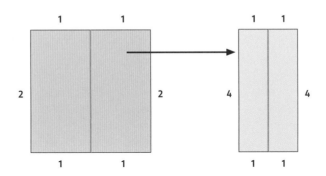

F

When twelve units are assembled following the system described in step D, the cube becomes pierced. The square holes separate the interlocked units, making it a little more difficult to visually assess the 'unders and overs' patterns at each vertex. Take care to glue the units together with a separation of exactly 90° between the edges.

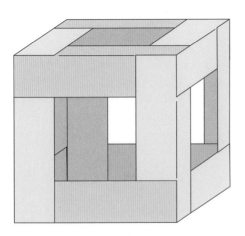

G

The unit can be made thinner, as below, turning a solid cube into a wire-frame cube. Depending on the weight of the card used, the fold down the centre of the units will keep them rigid, well beyond the 8 × 1 proportion shown here. Made with another (stronger) material, or by another process, the units can become almost unfeasibly skinny but remain strong.

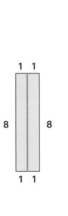

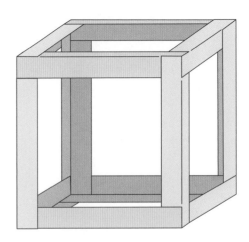

FIG. 2_12

2.3.3
Simplifying the iris

A

Here are the three tubes from 2.3.2B. Each was cut into four identical units, then reassembled to create a cube with iris-like rotational symmetry at each vertex. However, they need not be cut into four pieces.

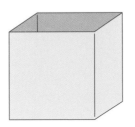 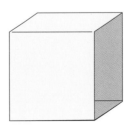 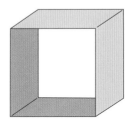

B

Here each tube is cut just once, each time parallel to the direction of the folds and across the centre of a face.

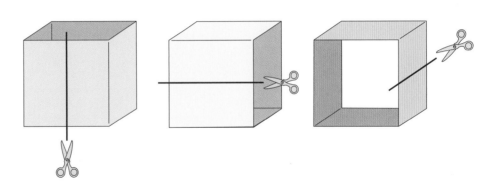

C

Opened out, the tubes are each 4 × 1 rectangles, with three squares placed centrally and half squares at the left and right edges.

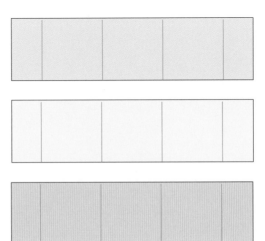

D

Despite the simplicity of the units, understanding how they weave together is a surprisingly complex puzzle. The good news is that no glue is required. Begin by arranging the units as shown, then, using the folds, quickly begin to create a cube-like form, allowing the squares to under- and overlap exactly as shown by the arrows. If the pattern is followed precisely, the same colour will appear on opposite faces, each corner will have iris-like rotational symmetry, and the whole structure will be very strongly locked.

To assemble the cube, arrange the three strips as shown, using small pieces of tape to hold the green strip to the yellow strip and the orange to the green. When the cube is assembled, remove the tape.

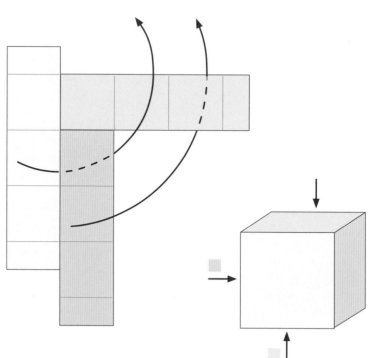

FIG. 2_13

2.3.3.1

Here is another way of simplifying the iris.

A

It is possible to cut each of the 4 × 1 strips (here shown small) into two pieces (shown bigger) so that there are six units, not three. Each unit becomes a 2 × 1 rectangle and has two folds.

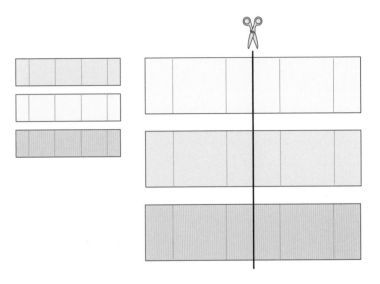

B

Here are the six units.

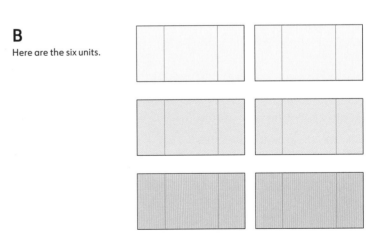

C

This six-piece cube was created by the author in the early 1980s. Somewhat against his wishes, it has become known eponymously as the Jackson Cube. The structure is so elemental that someone, somewhere must surely have made it previously, but despite research by academics and others into the history of origami (or 'paper folding' as it was known in English before the mid-twentieth century), no earlier reference has yet been found, in print at least.

This very simple unit is a portal into many rich areas of unit origami, also self-locking packaging nets, geometry kits and much more.

The author frequently teaches the unit...but rarely, if ever, tells his class how it should be assembled. Of all the structures in the book, this simple cube is perhaps the one that best exemplifies the need to think in three dimensions and to think symmetrically in three dimensions.

So...can you assemble it without step-by-step instructions (there are none in the book)?

What principles of three-dimensional symmetry did you apply when you assembled it?

What symmetries can you find in the distribution of the units around the faces, edges and vertices?

Can you take it apart and make it again quickly, to a plan?

What is the plan? Why did you use it and how?

Why does it hold together with such strength?

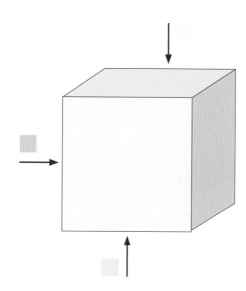

FIG. 2_14

2.3.4
Opening the iris

A

Instead of narrowing the unit to create square piercings in the middle of each face of the cube, it is possible to do the opposite – to widen the unit. We have seen that a square unit folded down the middle will create a solid cube. However, the height of the unit can be reduced from 2 to 1, while maintaining the same width. This reproportioning of the unit will create squares on both sides of the centre fold.

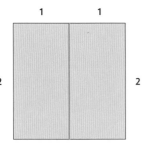

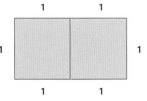

B

Make three units, as described in step A. Each unit has a central fold that divides it into square halves.

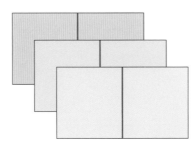

C

Arrange the units as shown, applying glue to two of the units. Glue them together as shown, being very careful to position the corner of one unit exactly in the centre of a square...

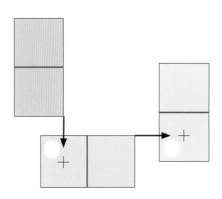

D

...like this. Finally, apply glue to the third unit to create a symmetrical arrangement of the three units, but now with a hole in the centre.

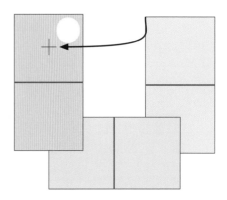

E

The assembled units can be imagined as sitting on three faces of a cube. A vertex of the cube will protrude between the units in the hole, and the folds on each unit will lie along the three edges that radiate away from the vertex. The iris has opened, but the three-dimensional rotational symmetry remains at the vertex.

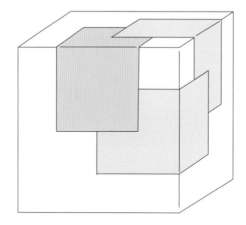

FIG. 2_15

F

As before, if one vertex can be made symmetrically, the locking system can be applied to a cube. Make twelve units, as shown.

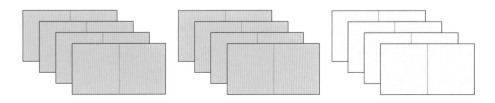

G

Interlock the units in the middle of each face, being careful to separate them by exactly 90°. There is nothing special about the specific proportion of the unit. Different proportions will shrink or enlarge the voids at each vertex. How narrow can the bands be made, but still create a strong cube?

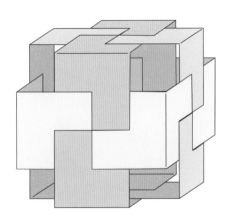

FIG. 2_16

H

As in 2.3.4C, the twelve units can be combined and simplified to create just three bands, one along each of the XYZ axes.

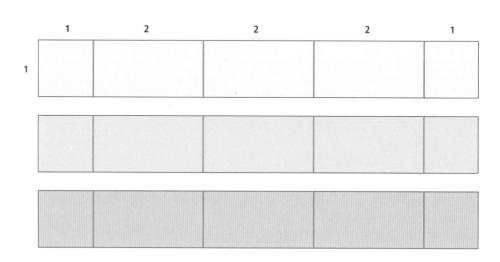

I

Notice the specific symmetrical 'under and over' pattern of the bands as they encircle the cube. The symmetry is simple, but also visually appealing.

Would there be any reason to cut the bands in half to create six units, in imitation of the Jackson Cube on page 80?

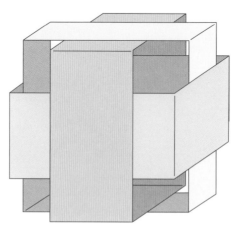

FIG. 2_17

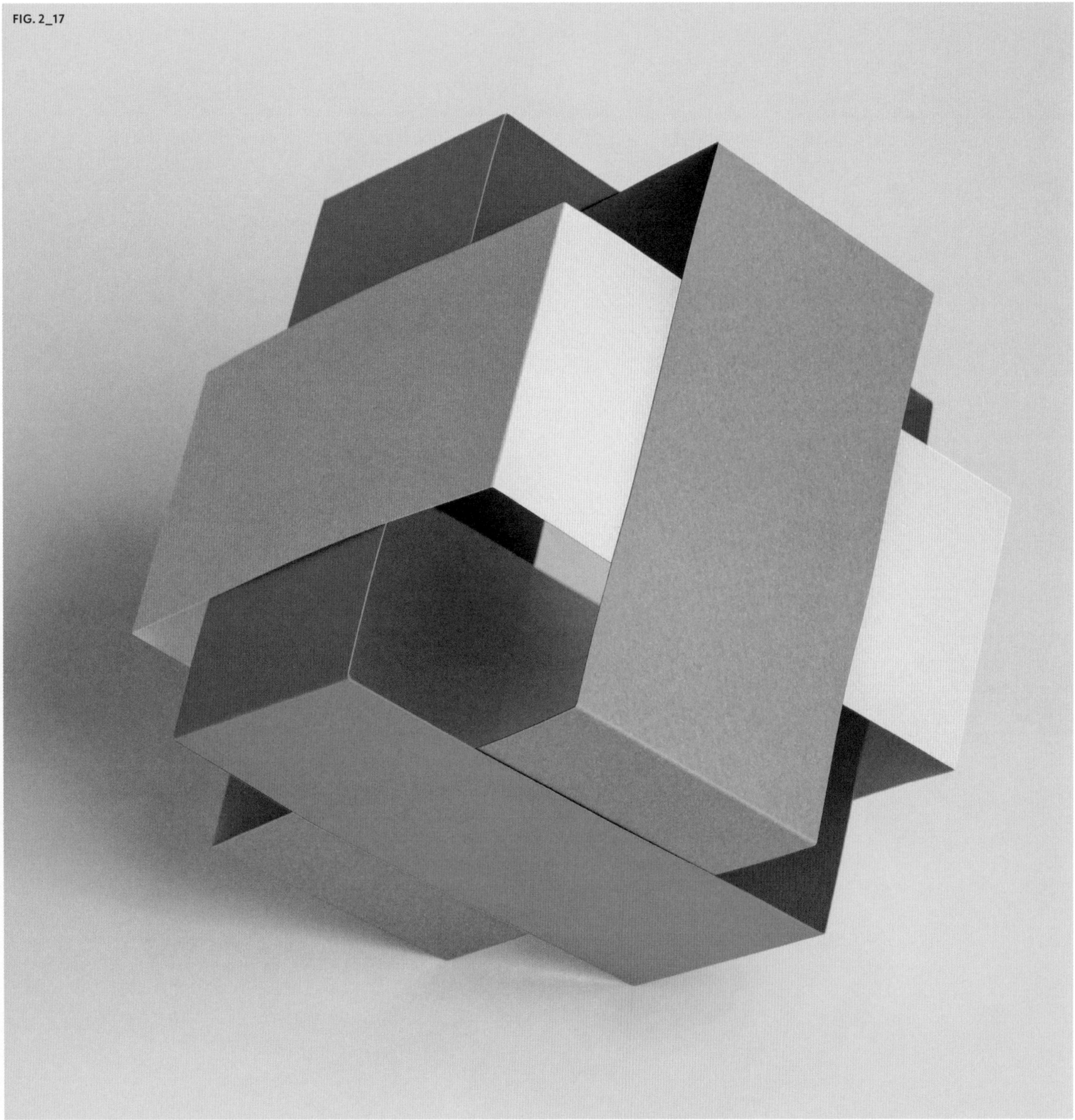

3

Symmetry on the XYZ Axes

Introduction

This chapter can be considered the heart of the book, and as much time as possible should be spent reading, making and absorbing its contents. The previous chapters gave many two- and three-dimensional examples of symmetry to help you better understand the characteristics and difficulties of working with both those dimensions. However, few of the examples were hardcore XYZ symmetry. This chapter, by contrast, focuses on XYZ symmetry.

It gives many examples for you to make from very simple, one-fold units. But don't be fooled. Many of these examples require a high degree of analytical understanding to assemble so that each of the units occupies each of the XYZ planes. With practice, the assembly will become simpler and quicker, but you will still probably have to put them together this way and that – at least, initially – to find the correct alignment that will create an example of XYZ symmetry. On some level, everything in this chapter is a puzzle (perhaps the whole book is a puzzle book). Solutions will be found only by experimenting with different alignments, while simultaneously analysing whether what you are making complies with the restrictions of three-dimensional symmetry. The combination of right-brain intuition with left-brain logic is always how designs of the highest order evolve.

Results are often beautiful and surprising, but also difficult to appreciate from one viewpoint. That is because they are designed fully in the third dimension and can thus be appreciated only in the third dimension.

Every moment you spend with this chapter will reward you, but before beginning to work from it, you are advised to absorb the contents of the book so far and to make as much as possible. That will ease your journey considerably.

3.1
Basic XYZ Symmetry

This is perhaps the simplest structure that can be made using identically folded units that occupy each of the XYZ directions. Once it is understood, many other structures can be made that derive from it.

Here is a reminder of how the XYZ Cartesian coordinate system looks.

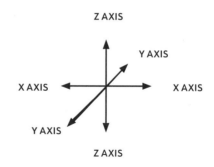

3.1.1
Using square units

A

Make three squares. Fold each in half, down the centre line. Note the black dots at the centre point of the squares.

B

The units are folded in half. Note the positions of the dots on the folded edges.

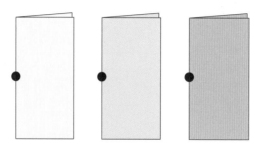

C

Bring two units into alignment, as shown, so that the dots touch each other. Spread glue on one half of one of the pieces, as shown. Be sure to align them accurately. (Hint: if you unfold both units, one square will lie exactly on top of the other.)

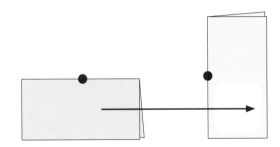

D

Now introduce the third unit, aligning the dot on the folded edge with the other two.

E

This is the magical part. Spread glue where shown and swivel the third unit behind the first unit, locking them together. The blue dots will touch (note: the blue dot on the right is on the rear corner only). The units will unfold and open to create the three-dimensional structure seen in the next step. Before applying the glue, it is recommended to rehearse the swivel.

F

This is the final result. Intriguingly, from any single angle, the structure is very difficult to understand. Even when turned around in the hand, it can be difficult to explain the relationship between the units. This is because the structure is constructed using three-dimensional symmetry so cannot be fully understood from any single (two-dimensional) viewpoint.

Note how the three folds follow the XYZ directions exactly, describing each of the six axes in 3.1. For all its simplicity, this is a complex, enigmatic and important structure. It can be considered a portal to understanding how to think and design in three dimensions. You are recommended to study it carefully before continuing.

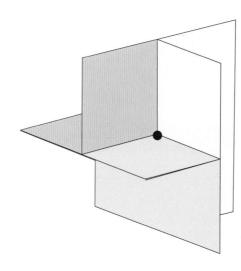

FIG. 3_1

3.1.2
Using rectangular units

A

Here we are using rectangles instead of squares. The exact proportion of the rectangles is unimportant, but here, each is 2 × 1. The dots are in the centre of each rectangle. Fold the units in half.

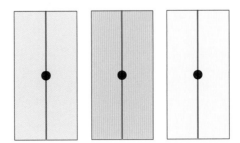

B

Here are the three folded units.

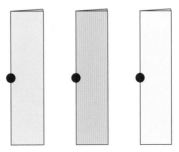

C

Align two units as shown, allowing the dots to meet exactly. Hold them together with a little glue, as shown. Be careful to make them lie exactly perpendicular to each other.

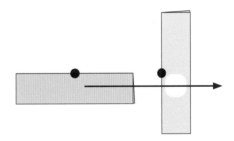

D

Introduce the third unit, bringing the third dot to meet the other two. Hold it to the second (horizontal) unit with a little glue.

E

Swivel the third unit behind the first, allowing the blue dots to touch (note: the dot on the right is on the rear edge). Hold them together with glue. This will unfold all three units to create the final structure.

F

The structure is complete. It exhibits the same set of characteristics as the previous example, but the extra length of its spans means that it is a little easier to comprehend from any one viewpoint.

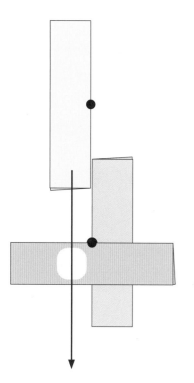

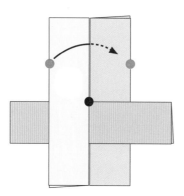

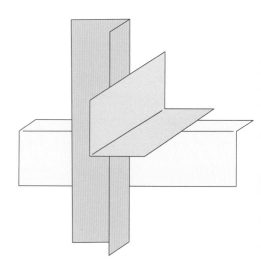

FIG. 3_2

3.1.2.1

Here is another way to use rectangular units.

A

This time, the three 2 × 1 rectangles have
a centre fold placed parallel to the short sides.
Fold each in half. Note the dots.

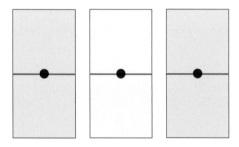

B

These are the units folded in half. As always,
remember the position of the dots.

C

Can you remember what to do? The technique
for joining the units is the same each time; it is
just the proportion of the units that will change.
As before, bring the units together so that two
dots touch. Hold them together with glue.

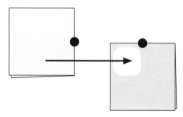

D

Introduce a third unit, again aligning the dots.

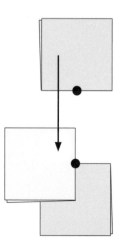

E

Glue the first unit to the third, bringing the blue dots together. The units will unfold to create the final three-dimensional structure.

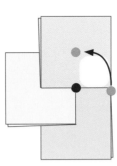

F

This is the result. As always, the structure is somewhat enigmatic and difficult to understand from one viewpoint.

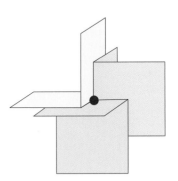

FIG. 3_3

3.1.3
Square and rectangular variations

A

When a square has a centre fold, there is no
reason to place the dots at the centre point
of the square. Here the dots are towards the
bottom of the centre line. Assemble the three
units as before. The asymmetric placement
of the dots makes the assembly a little more
complex. Think before you glue.

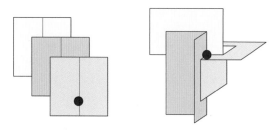

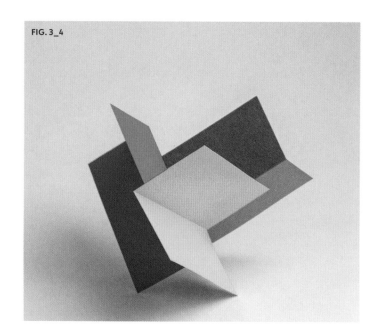

FIG. 3_4

B

The fold itself need not be placed
symmetrically, down the centre line of the
square. Here it is towards the right-hand edge.
The dots are at the mid-point of the fold.
Assemble the units as before.

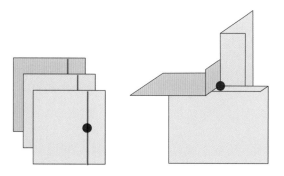

FIG. 3_5

C

Combining the two variations opposite, both the fold and the dot are off-centre. Assemble the units as before.

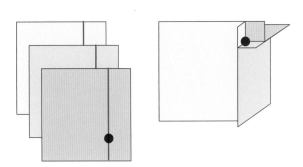

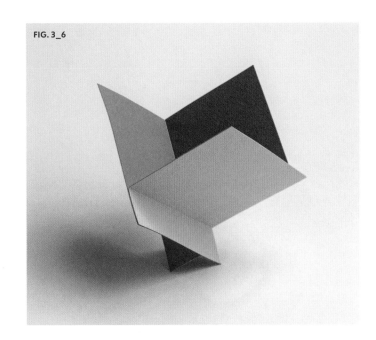

FIG. 3_6

D

The same variations can be performed with rectangles. Here are two of them. In this first example, the fold is dropped towards the bottom edge. Note that the dots are at 45° from a vertex. Assemble the units as before.

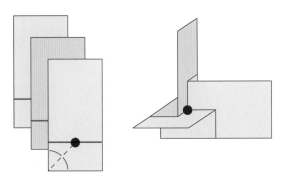

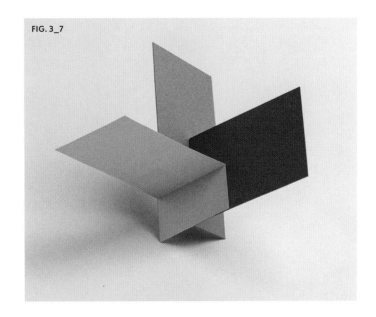

FIG. 3_7

E

This is a second variation, this time using a long centre line with the dots 45° from a vertex. Assemble as before.

There are many other possible variations. How many can you find? Are some easier to assemble than others? Why are some more difficult than others to assemble? Is an example that is more complex to assemble more aesthetic to look at, or, in your opinion, is there no relationship between complexity and beauty? What might happen if the unit were not a square or a rectangle, but a rhombus, or even a triangle or a circle?

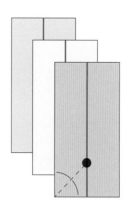

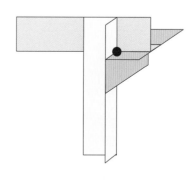

FIG. 3_8

From an XYZ Vertex to an XYZ Cube

The previous section explained how to create an XYZ vertex. When several vertices are put together, they create a cube. Each unit is an edge of the cube, connecting two vertices.

Two different cube structures can be made. One uses a fold that runs along a rectangular unit in the long direction; the other uses a fold that runs along a rectangular unit in the short direction. Both are described below.

3.2.1
A unit with a long fold

A

Here is the assembled three-unit vertex made in 3.1.3E (opposite).

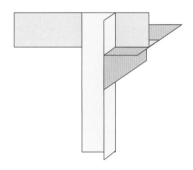

B

Each unit is a 2 × 1 rectangle with a fold on the longer axis.

C

Imagine joining two units...

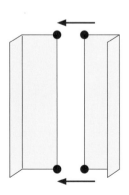

D

...like this.

E

The result would be a square with two folds, each on a quarter line.

F

We can assemble the three units to create a vertex. Note the position of the dots.

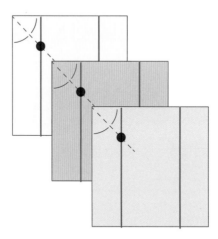

G

This is the result. The three folds away from the vertex play no part in the three-unit structure. However, they can be used to create other vertices if more units are added to the structure.

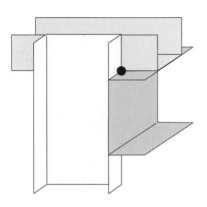

FIG. 3_9

H

To add more units, each unit must be part of four vertices. Each unit is a face.

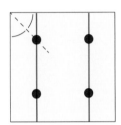

I

Make six units, each with folds along the quarter lines. Add four dots as shown, to mark where a unit will meet other units at four separate vertices.

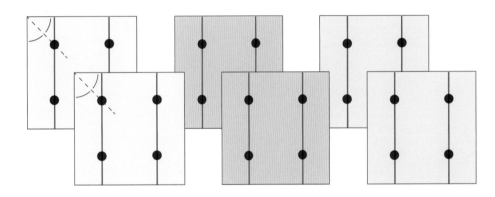

J

Assemble the units to create a solid cube with elaborate edges and vertices. Arrange the units so that units of the same colour occupy opposing faces.

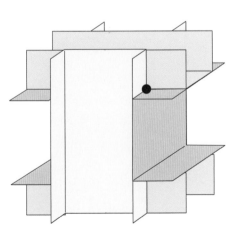

FIG. 3_10

3.2.1.1

The units can also be made narrower.

A

When two narrower units are placed on the same plane such that the four dots describe a square, the centre becomes a void. The effect of this is to create a cube with square piercings on every face. The units here are 4 × 1, but any unit longer than 2 × 1 will create a void. The narrower the unit, the larger the void.

B

Here is the final result. Being pierced, the structure is much less massive-looking than the earlier solid cube. Note how the four units of each of the three colours follow an XYZ direction.

What is the maximum length the units can be before the cube has no strength? Can a cube be subdivided into smaller cubes using the same XYZ locking system, or can separately made cubes be joined to make a hyper-cube?

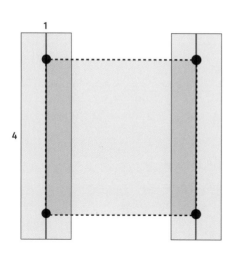

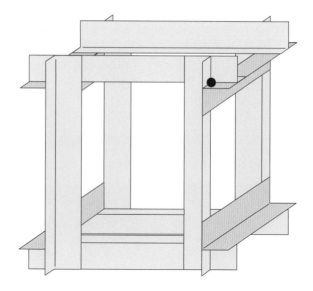

FIG. 3_11

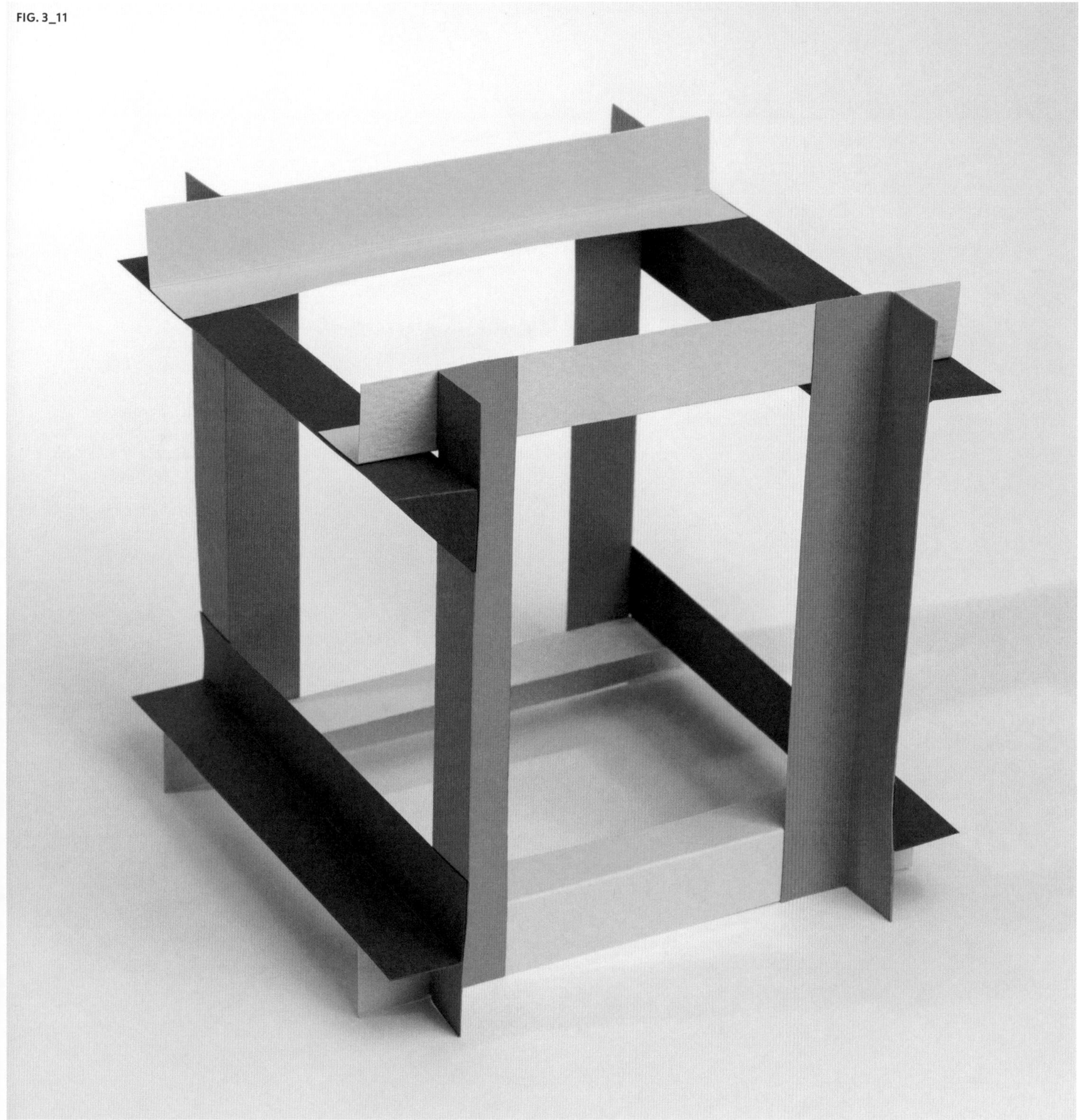

3.2.2
A unit with a short fold

A

This vertex is the same as the one shown in fig. 3_7.

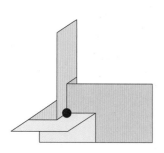

B

The fold is one quarter of the distance across the unit. The dot is in the middle of the fold.

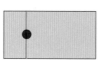

C

Two units can be placed together...

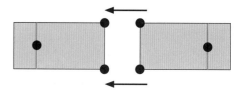

D

...like this.

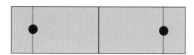

E

Each unit is now 4 × 1 and the folds are one eighth of the way across the unit from the short sides. The dots are in the middle of the folds.

F

Make twelve units, four each of three colours.

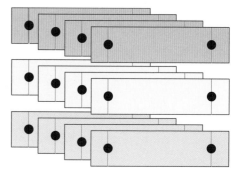

G

The cube is simple to assemble. However, whereas the cube in the previous section had edges defined by long folds, in this cube, there are no folds along the edges. The edges are defined by flat planes. This has the inevitable effect of making the cube a little weak, but the result is fascinating and unexpected.

If the units were widened so that the pierced faces became solid, the units would lock in the same way as the solid cube in 3.2.1 (see fig. 3_10). Essentially, we would have made the same cube again, but beginning with a short fold, not a long fold. That's a strange result.

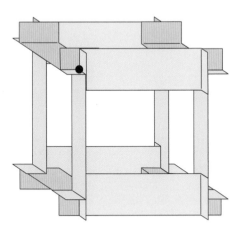

FIG. 3_12

3.3
XYZ Symmetry with Diagonal Folds

Sections 3.1 and 3.2 showed how examples of XYZ symmetry could be created with folds that were parallel to the edges of a square or rectangle. This section will show what happens when the fold is at an angle to the edges.

3.3.1
The basic example

A

Make three squares. Fold each square along a diagonal. Note the dots at the centre points of the squares.

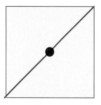 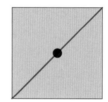 

B

Bring two units together as shown, aligning the two dots. The glue will hold the units together.

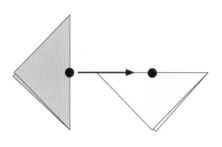

C

Add a third unit as shown, again aligning the dots.

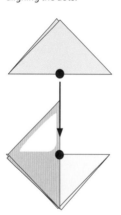

D

Finally, add glue to the third unit as shown, then twist the assembly into three dimensions, aligning the blue dots...

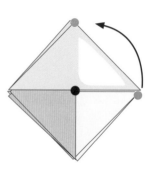

E

...like this. There are no loose vertices or planes, so the form is particularly rigid. The simplicity of the construction creates an archetypal twisted form that is attractive, strong and practical. Note how each of the three folds occupies one of the XYZ directions, and how, despite the 45° diagonal folds, they intersect at the centre point at 90°.

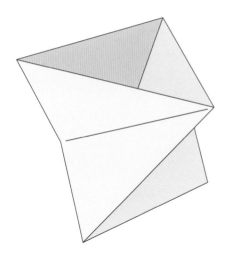

FIG. 3_13

3.3.2
Rectangular variation

A

A diagonal can also be placed on a rectangle. The example shown here is 2 × 1. Again, the dots are at the centre points of the folds.

B

Bring two units together, as shown. Note that the area to be glued is small and irregularly shaped. The dots will touch.

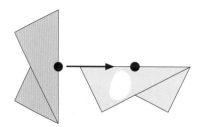

C

Introduce a third unit, as before.

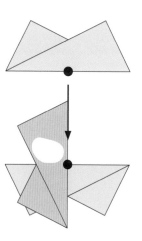

D

Apply glue to the third unit, then twist the assembly into the third dimension, aligning the blue dots.

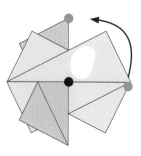

E

This is the result. The twisting has created a form that is both regular (the planes intersect at 90°) and irregular (the perimeter silhouette is unusually random). It's an interesting mix of the methodical and the chaotic.

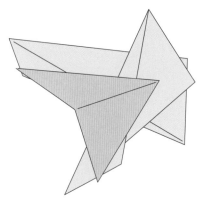

FIG. 3_14

3.3.3
Further variations

A

An angled fold need not run along a diagonal, connecting opposite vertices. In this example, the fold is at 45° through the centre point of the unit. The dots are at the mid-point of the folds.

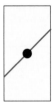  

B

Glue two units together, as shown. Note that for the first time, the units are aligning in an anticlockwise direction. In previous examples, they aligned in a clockwise direction. The reason is to keep you alert through many similar constructions! Even a simple change like this can be difficult to assimilate.

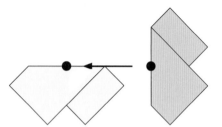

C

Introduce a third unit.

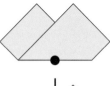

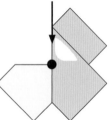

D

Finally, apply glue to the third unit and twist the assembly into the third dimension, aligning the blue dots.

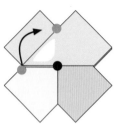

E

The structure is surprisingly light in appearance, even though it has the same geometry as 3.3.1.

What would happen if the rectangle grew to a lengthy strip? Could a second angled fold along the strip combine with others to create more vertices and, eventually, a polyhedron? If so, which polyhedron? This way of creating a vertex by aligning diagonal folds offers many interesting possibilities to explore.

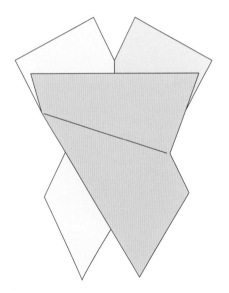

FIG. 3_15

A

In this variation, the fold connects the middle of a side with a vertex. The dots are at the mid-points of the folds.

B

As always, align the dots. Note the unusual shape of the area to be glued.

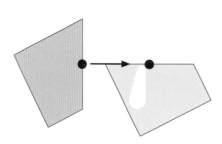

C

Align a third unit, dot to dot.

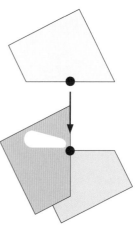

D

Apply glue to the third unit, then swivel the first unit as shown, aligning the blue dots. The three units will unfold to create the final form.

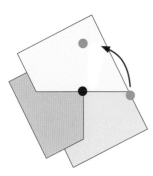

E

Although a little random-looking, the form is unusual because it stands on three vertices, creating a structure with a pleasingly lightweight aesthetic. Can you design other structures that lock in the same way, and that stand on vertices?

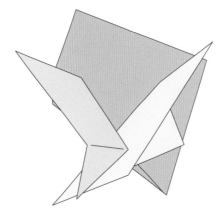

FIG. 3_16

A

Now the fold connects the mid-points of two adjacent sides. As always, the dots are in the middle of the folds.

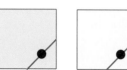
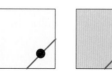

B

Align two units, as shown. Note the small triangular area to be glued.

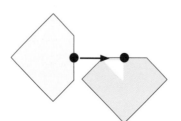

C

Align the third unit, dot to dot.

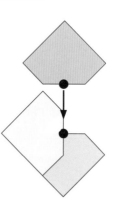

D

Apply glue to the third unit, then swivel the first unit as shown, aligning the blue dots. The three units will unfold to create the final form.

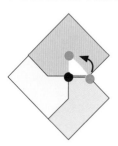

E

Perhaps unexpectedly for a form in which the three units have minimal contact with one another, the form is not open and thrusting, but ground-hugging. What would happen if the same folds were made on a 2 × 1 strip, not a square? Should the strips hug the ground or rise up? Squares are the simplest polygon with which to begin a series of experiments, but sometimes, more interesting results are found by using strips, or even other polygons. If you have an idea, make it. These simple forms take just minutes to construct and cost pennies, but always seem to yield something unexpected. Just as importantly, they give great practice at thinking and designing in three dimensions.

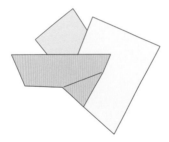

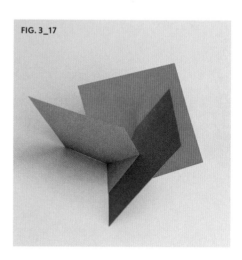

FIG. 3_17

A

Here, the fold passes through the centre point of a square at an angle of 22.5° to the horizontal. The angle is unimportant, but set as it is, it will create four adjacent triangles at the perimeter, each with angles of 90-45-45°, when the fold is made.

B

Align two units, as shown. Note the irregularly shaped area to be glued.

67.5°

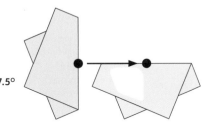

C

Align the third unit as shown, dot to dot.

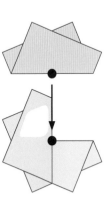

D

Apply glue to the third unit, then swivel the first unit as shown, aligning the blue dots. The three units will unfold to create the final form.

E

This is the final form. By having the folds avoid all the vertices, the form has a large number of 90° vertices flying in all directions (how many?), in the manner of a three-dimensional explosion. Yet this seemingly intricate result is no more complex to construct than the other XYZ forms depicted in this section.

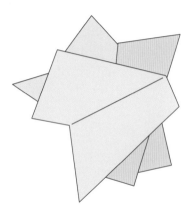

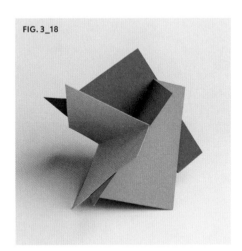

FIG. 3_18

A

Finally in this section, a puzzle. If you have made many of the examples that precede this one, you will be familiar with how the units join. The units in this final example are 2 × 1 rectangles, with a fold that touches a vertex and that crosses the rectangle at 45°. The dots are at the mid-points of the folds.

B

Here are the units.

This is the puzzle: the units can join in two different ways. One way is ground-hugging. The other thrusts the units upwards. Can you find both ways to join them?

The photograph below shows the two ways the units can join. The results create forms that are very different: one horizontal, the other vertical.

Now go back to some of the other examples in this section. Make the same units again and see if you can find a second way to join them so that the final form differs from the first. Sometimes this is possible, sometimes it is not. The key idea is to understand that the three units can be assembled clockwise or anticlockwise. Sometimes the forms are the same whichever way they join, and sometimes they are different.

What are the rules for creating forms that are identical or different? Can you exaggerate the differences by redesigning the shapes of the card and the folds? Sometimes a very simple answer is there, but it can take much careful three-dimensional thinking to tease it out. These supposedly ultra-simple units can take time, effort and much head-scratching to understand fully. They can also create unexpected and beautiful results. Ultimately, they are perfect exercises to help you think and design in the third dimension.

FIG. 3_19

FIG. 3_20

3.4
One-piece Twists

A fascinating diversion from assembling multi-unit examples of XYZ symmetry is to re-create them from just one piece of card. This technique is quicker, easier and often stronger than the technique given previously, but works only in specific circumstances.

3.4.1
Basic examples

A

This is the unit made in 3.3.1A. The fold connects opposite vertices so that the four sides remain unfolded. This placement of the fold means that any of the sides can be connected to other units, horizontally or vertically, or both.

B

When three units are connected in a line, this is the result. Note the glue tab and that whereas the three vertical folds are valleys, the three diagonal folds are mountains (or the opposite way around, if the card is viewed from the reverse).

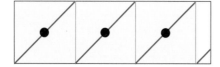

C

The three sections can be folded up and glued together to look like this. It is an exact copy of 3.3.1E.

D

The inverted pyramids on the top side and also on the underside have 3 × 90° vertices inside at the apex, which means that the corner of a cube or cuboid will nest exactly inside, as shown. Complex three-dimensional networks of cubes and/or cuboids can be joined in this way to resemble molecules or crystals.

What happens if rows of three squares are stacked one on another, but made from one sheet of card?

What happens if there are four squares in a row? Can there be more than four?

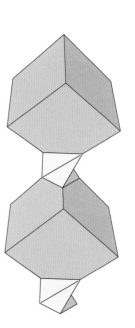

A

A beautiful variation is to make a diagonal fold across a rectangle proportioned 1:√2 (1:1.414). Create a row of four rectangles and add a glue tab.

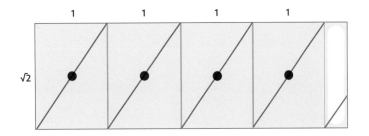

B

Glue the tab to create a tube, then twist the tube in the manner described in 3.4.1B and C, to create the form seen here.

Careful analysis of the different lengths of the different edges will reveal that the form describes a perfect cube. That's a big surprise and a wonderful example of how geometry can sometimes create forms that seem to have been discovered, rather than contrived. Geometry has the ability to create forms that have a rightness, an inevitability. Some designers would consider this the highest form of design aesthetic.

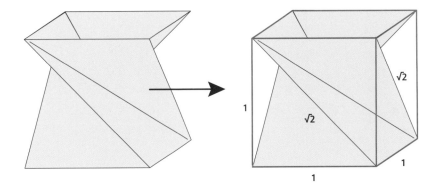

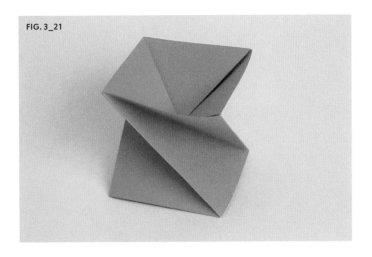

FIG. 3_21

3.4.2
Twisted variations

A

The critical factor when designing a twisted form is to calculate the angle of the diagonal fold in relation to the number of rectangular panels across the card. In the example shown here, the key angle of the diagonal should be 60° to the horizontal, when the form is to have six panels, or six sides. This is because the angle from a vertex to the centre point on a hexagon (a polygon with six sides) is 60°.

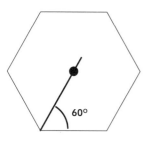

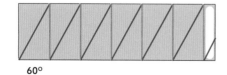

60°

B

When the tube is made, simultaneously twist all the folds...

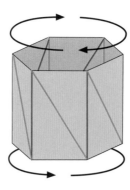

C

...like this. The result will be a double-layered *flat* hexagon, not a twisted, three-dimensional tube. Flat? Yes. The reason is that the angles of the flat hexagonal discs re-create the angles inside the flat hexagon seen in step A.

To create a six-sided three-dimensional tube, the angle must be increased from 60° to 61, 62, 63°...and more. The greater the angle above 60°, the more elongated the tube will become.

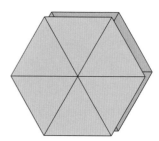

A

An alternative way to create a twisted tube is to keep the angle of 60°, but reduce the number of rectangular panels from six, to five, to four, to three, as shown here, thus reducing the number of sides from a hexagon (six sides), to create a pentagon (five sides), a square (four sides) and an equilateral triangle (three sides). The fewer the sides, the more upright the tube will stand.

Experiment with the angles of the diagonal in relation to the number of sides. The greater the number of sides, the more difficult it becomes to twist the tubes. Sometimes, a little patience is required, but with practice, you will acquire the knack of making them quickly.

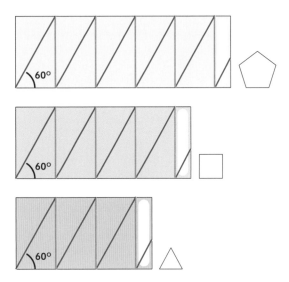

B

Here are the three polygonal twists. What would happen if, instead of progressively decreasing the number of sides from six to three, the number of sides were progressively increased to seven and above? Would the card still twist, or would something else happen?

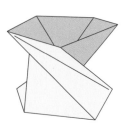
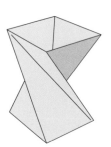
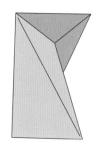

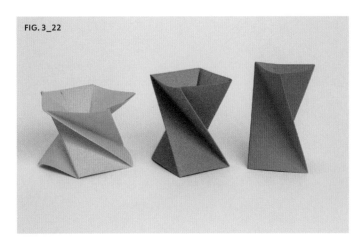

FIG. 3_22

4

Exploring Wider Concepts of XYZ Symmetry

Introduction

If you have flicked non-committally backwards and forwards through the preceding chapters, perhaps making one or two pieces, but generally saying to yourself, 'I understand, I understand,' you should possibly not be reading this. Please go back and make more pieces. The way to learn how to think and design in the third dimension is not to look, but to *make*. The more you make, the more you will understand and the more fluency you will gain in thinking and working truly in three dimensions. There is no short cut, no magic trick.

This final chapter assumes you have made a good number of the pieces in the preceding chapters, so it does not need to hold your hand, step by step, to help you assemble the units. It is expected that you have already learned the principles of thinking and designing in the third dimension and therefore do not need detailed instructions. That said, many of the assemblies here will still be puzzles and, despite the simplicity of the units, may take time and effort to put together. You will occasionally need to think long and deep, but those moments are why you are here. It is always when solving problems that you learn the most.

In the process of learning how to assemble the units, you may well find alternative solutions to those shown here. Every unit can be joined to others in a multiplicity of ways, some self-evident, others difficult to find – if, indeed, they exist at all. Not all hunts end in a triumphant success.

The purpose of this final chapter is to ease you out of the book and into designing your own pieces by thinking three-dimensionally in whatever materials, for whatever reason. Are you ready for it?

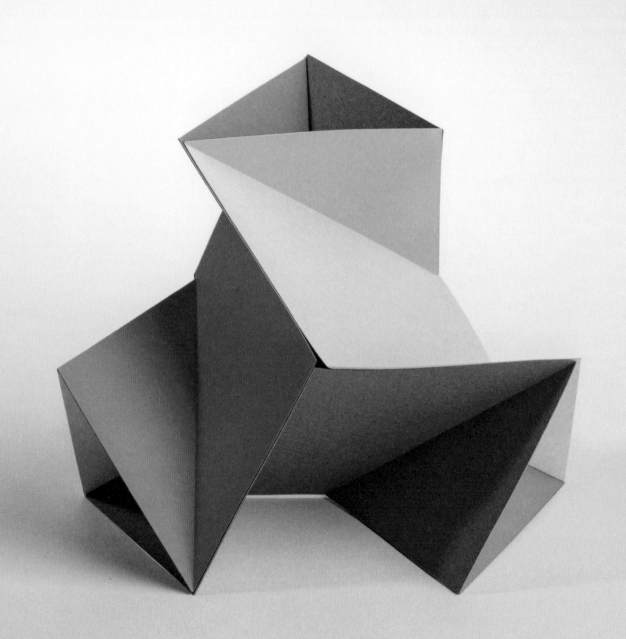

4.1
One-fold Solutions

Gathered here, for ease of reference, are the one-fold XYZ-symmetry units from the previous chapter. If you have made only a few of them, it would be helpful to make a few more before beginning to make the multi-fold examples that follow. What you see here is not a complete set of possibilities. Consider these questions:

In what other ways might a fold be placed on a square?

Other than a square or a 2 × 1 rectangle, which four-sided quadrilaterals might be useful?

Must all three units be identical?

Which other polygons can be used?

Can you make these examples in other materials?

Do you have a favourite? Why that particular one?

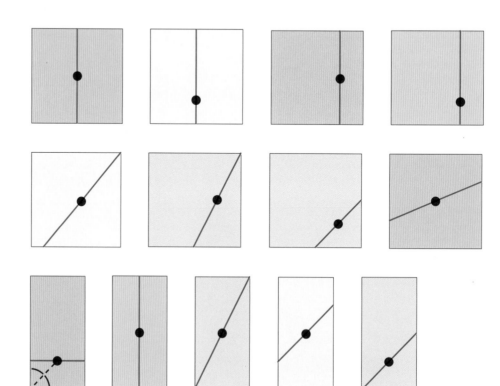

4.2.1
Three-unit example

Two folds are placed across adjacent corners. The puzzle is to place three of them together in a symmetrical way using both folds. The solution given here (there might be others) is an example not of XYZ symmetry, but of rotational symmetry, around a central point.

Can four and more units be added to the rotation?

What happens if the folds are made smaller?

x3

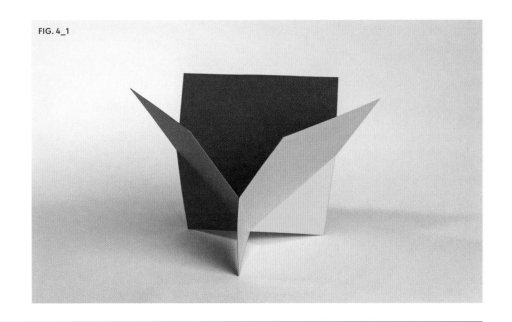

FIG. 4_1

4.2.2
Six-unit example

Surprisingly, this simple unit will create a cube when six are glued together. The key idea is not to glue a triangle on one unit to a triangle on another, but to glue a triangle on one unit to a corner on another unit *without* a triangle. This will set up the possibility of joining six units using XYZ symmetry. It's a simple but pleasing construction.

What will happen if you try to make a cube from a 2 × 1 rectangle using the same XYZ symmetry?

Which other forms can you create, perhaps gluing only triangles to triangles?

x6

FIG. 4_2

4.3
Three-fold Solutions

4.3.1
Three-plus units example

This is a doubly unusual example. First, it can be made from any number of units greater than two. Second, once assembled, the form can be inverted (popped inside out) to create a very different three-dimensional form. The 'popping' to and from is fun to do. Interestingly, neither of the two possible forms dominates the other; they are of equal importance.

Why do three units not use all the folds, but four and more do?

Is there a maximum number of units that can be used?

What will happen if the square becomes a rectangle and the joining pattern is repeated at the other end, with two, four or five units?

x>2

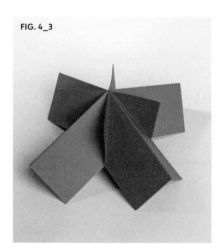
FIG. 4_3

4.3.2
Three-unit example: no. 1

Three units can be assembled in strict accordance with XYZ symmetry to create a simple, box-like, three-sided inverted pyramid. Can you see other ways to join the units, perhaps in a rotational pattern? This unit can seem to be one of the least versatile in the chapter, but spending time trying to join a number of them in many different ways will reveal unexpected results. The only rule, as always, is to ensure that each unit joins to the others in the same way.

x3

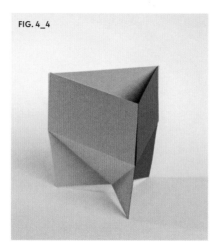
FIG. 4_4

4.3.3
Three- and four-unit example

Some units are more fun to play with than others. This is one of the most enjoyable, from which many different forms can be made, mostly with three or four units. The small squares on different units can be glued together, as can the pairs of triangles. These two different ways of joining the units create very different forms, and there are several variations within each system.

How many ways can you find to join two units?

Can you successfully join more than four units?

Are all the symmetry patterns rotational, or can you also find some XYZ symmetry patterns?

x3

FIG. 4_5

4.3.4
Twelve-unit example

This is one of the few constructions in the book that will hold together without glue, making it an example of unit origami, sometimes called modular origami. It was first documented by the origami master Kenneth Kawamura in 1977, since when it has become popularly known as the Butterfly Ball, for the reason that if it is made from thin origami paper, tossed into the air and swatted, the units will separate and flutter to the ground like butterflies. The twelve-unit polyhedron is a cuboctahedron, with the triangular faces indented. It is an excellent example of how XYZ patterns of symmetry can interlock units in interesting and complex patterns. Can you think how colour can be used to emphasize the symmetry? How many colours do you need to colour the surface symmetrically: two, three, four or six? Are there different solutions?

The black arrow indicates that the centre point of the paper should be pushed downwards, enabling the three folds to form around it.

There are other ways to assemble a number of units using just three or four of them and glue. How many ways can you find? Do they use XYZ or rotational symmetry, or both?

x12, x3, x4

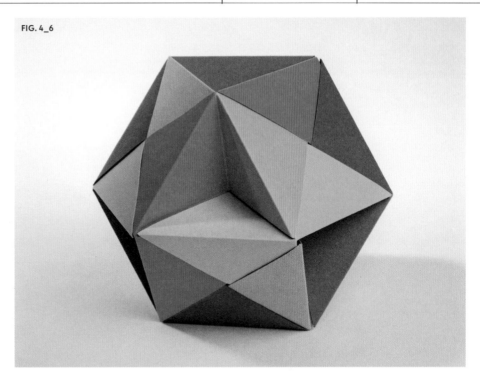

FIG. 4_6

FIG. 4_7

4.3.5
Three-unit example: no. 2

Rectangular units can take a folded motif used on a square and repeat it. The motif used here was first seen in the previous chapter – simply a diagonal fold across a square – repeated one above the other, each a mirror image of the other. They join in the same way as before to create a classic example of XYZ symmetry, but now two examples are stacked, one above the other. The horizontal fold separates the two twists. All the polygons are triangles, and when joined to each other, the cross-section is also triangular. With everything being triangular, the final form has exceptional strength; it will not bend, twist or deform without an unusual amount of pressure.

Can the form be strengthened or weakened by changing the proportion of the rectangle of card?

Can further twists be added to the stack? What is the limit?

Can different angles be used on each section of the stack?

FIG. 4_8

x3

4.4.1
Two- and three-unit example

For the first time in the book, two units can be brought together. The result is a symmetrical form, but one unit is on top of the other, so the arrangement of the units is not symmetrical. In the strictest sense, is this a symmetrical form? You decide!

Three units can also be joined by gluing together the trapezoids. More units can be added so that the units become increasingly squashed together around the centre point.

The photograph below shows the two-unit version; the QR code links to a video showing the very different-looking three-unit version.

x2, x3

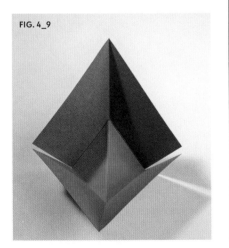

FIG. 4_9

4.4.2
Three-unit example: no. 1

This classic unit should perhaps have appeared in an earlier chapter. Three units interlock well to create an inverted vertex. Of course, if the square were elongated to become a 2 × 1 rectangle, there would be space to repeat the V-fold at the opposite end. More units interlocked at that second location would create a cube.

How many units would be needed to make a cube? Why? Is each unit a face, a vertex or an edge? What coloration would be symmetrical? Is the structure using XYZ symmetry?

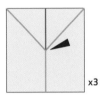

x3

FIG. 4_10

4.4.3
Six-unit example: no. 1

Here is another of the rare unit origami examples, which, pleasingly, do not require glue. When the units are fully interlocked, they hold together with remarkable strength. It is a wonderful example of multiple XYZ symmetry and will repay careful study. It was first created by the origami master Robert E. Neale in the early 1960s, and deserves its reputation as one of the greatest unit origami designs.

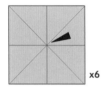

x6

Fold the six units to this star shape. Ensure that the folds are made crisply. On each unit, draw (or scribble) four circles on to the four marked triangular surfaces, as shown. Assemble the units by sliding the triangles with drawn circles fully inside the triangles without the circles. Eventually, with this method, the form will complete itself and no circle will be visible. The assembly is simple to understand, but you may need an extra pair of hands to hold the units in place.

To achieve the illusion of three interpenetrating squares, how many colours do you need?

How are the colours distributed?

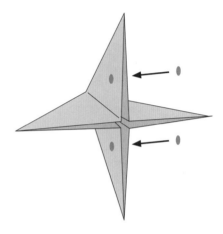

FIG. 4_11

4.4.4
Six-unit example: no. 2

This is another classic unit origami design by Kenneth Kawamura, from the 1970s (see also 4.3.4). No glue is required, although a few spots here and there will certainly help it to hold together with greater strength. In many ways, it is similar to the design opposite.

Fold the unit as shown. It is the inversion of the star unit opposite. Each unit is the other, popped inside out. Draw circles on four triangles, as shown.

As with the star units, the units are locked together by placing the triangles with circles under the triangles with no circles. When complete, no circle will be visible; if you can see one, the locking pattern is not symmetrical and the strength of the assembled form will be severely compromised. The assembly is delicate and you may need an extra pair of hands. Even when assembled, it will not be very strong.

Can you list the similarities and differences between this example and the one opposite?

How many colours are needed to create a symmetrically coloured surface?

Is it possible to lock fewer than six units together symmetrically and without glue? (Hint: try using just two units.)

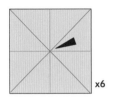

x6

FIG. 4_12

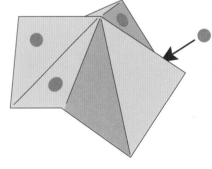

4.4.5
Three-unit example: no. 2

Here is another of the XYZ interlocking systems that features a three-sided pyramid. The distribution of mountain and valley folds is subtle, so be sure to follow the distribution of the folds carefully. It is also possible to interlock just two units.

Can more than three units be interlocked?

What will happen if the square becomes a 2 × 1 rectangle and the 'V' is repeated at both ends?

Can the 'V' be repeated on two neighbouring sides of a square?

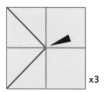

x3

FIG. 4_13

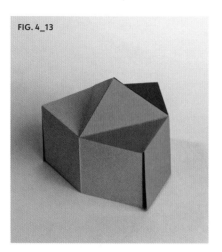

4.4.6
Six-unit example: no. 3

This unit is so simple that it could be taught in a kindergarten class! Despite its simplicity, it is a wonderful example of basic XYZ symmetry, in which the units fit together almost intuitively. The ease of construction elevates the piece to classic status.

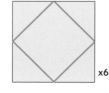

x6

How many colours are needed to create a symmetrically coloured surface?

Can the units be assembled if the folds separate, become smaller and move towards the vertices?

Will the same system work using the three vertices of an equilateral triangle or the six vertices of a hexagon?

Can the folded square be split into two mirror-image V-folds at the ends of a 2 × 1 rectangle?

What forms can be made when paper triangles are folded and glued together in the same way as the six paper squares are folded and glued, shown here?

FIG. 4_14

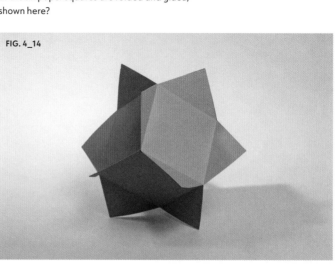

4.5.1
Three-unit example: no. 1

This unit is very similar to the example immediately preceding it, 4.4.6. It contains an additional fold across the middle, splitting the central square into two triangles and thus creating two planes. The effect is to reduce the six units used in 4.4.6 to three. The solid form is called a hexahedron.

Can the same gluing pattern be maintained if the unit is stretched to become a 2 × 1 rectangle?

If stretched, should the horizontal fold be along the short or long axis of the rectangle, or perhaps either?

4.5.2
Combining different units: no. 1

It is sometimes possible to combine different units into the same assembly. Usually, this happens when assembling a number of identical units creates an unstable form and a second, different unit helps to hold the form together in a stable and tidy way. This assembly technique creates many interesting possibilities for using units of different colours to create a variety of symmetrical patterns.

In this example, four identical units are made, two of one colour and two of another. There is just one unit folded differently, a different colour from the four identical units.

Glue the four units together, alternating the colours. The pyramidic top will not remain closed, and looks unresolved. Fold the different unit and, from inside the assemblage, push its four triangular fins up inside the four triangles. It will stabilize the triangles. A little glue may be required. It may be necessary to trim a sliver off the bottom edges of the extra piece so that it fits inside the other four.

If you have some experimental forms that did not hold together, review them and see if the addition of a different unit will help to stabilize them. A surprising number of so-called failures can be rescued in this way.

x3

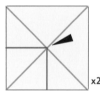 x2

 x2

 x1

FIG. 4_15

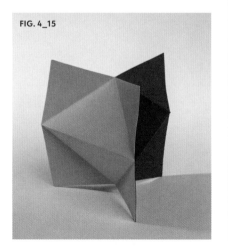

FIG. 4_16

4.5.3
Combining different units: no. 2

The four identical units – two of one colour and two of another – are unstable and untidy when glued together. The two additional and different units create a total of eight XYZ vertices when woven in and out of the unstable areas. The fully assembled form will hold together, but may benefit from a few spots of glue.

The use of colour is interesting and subtle if the surface is to have a symmetrical distribution of the two colours. Try different ways of interweaving the extra units to achieve a symmetrical effect.

Without using the extra units, can you find other ways of interlocking the four units to create different forms?

 x2   x2   x2

FIG. 4_17

4.5.4
Six units: no. 1

The 45° fold is a staple of symmetrical constructions. This example is beautiful and contains a wealth of interesting XYZ symmetries across its fascinating structure.

The solid form at the centre, surprisingly perhaps, is a cube.

The strip can be elongated, with parallel 45° folds across every square division along the strip – so, for example, a 6 × 1 strip would have six parallel folds at 45°. The effect of interweaving many identical strips is to create an XYZ network of cubes that touch vertex to vertex, held solidly in place by the twisted connections. If you are looking for a super-complex project to make, this is a worthwhile candidate.

How should the form be coloured to create a symmetrically coloured surface?

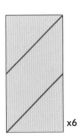 x6

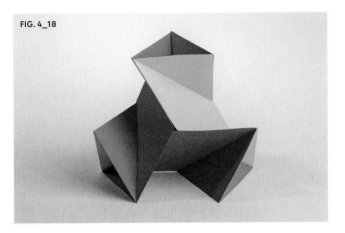

FIG. 4_18

4.5.5
Six units: no. 2

This is the same as the previous example, 4.5.4, except that the 2 × 1 strip has been stretched to 4 × 1, separating the two 45° folds.

The effect is to open the solid cube so that it assumes the form of a tetrahedron. This transformation of a cube into a tetrahedron is beautiful and surprising. Who would have expected that a cube made from six squares and a tetrahedron made from four triangles were so closely related? Interestingly, note how the original 2 × 1 units created the faces of a cube, but the 4 × 1 units create the edges of a tetrahedron.

Why would this face-to-edge transformation happen?

Are there other face-to-edge transformations?

Can other solids be opened and transformed by stretching or compressing the units?

x6

4.5.6
Infinite plane

Whereas the dozens of other examples in the book have all made finite three-dimensional solids, this example of XYZ symmetry creates an infinite plane.

Three units create an inverted pyramid form seen many times in the book, but a second twist on the same unit, made with the opposite and parallel fold, corrects the tendency of the card to curl around into a three-dimensional form. This second twist enables the unit to repeat across a flat, infinite plane.

To see the effect, it is recommended to use at least twenty-four units: eight units of one colour, eight of a second colour and eight of a third.

The obvious question: is this infinite plane construction unique, or are there others?

If there are others, is the key to repeat a fold on a unit, but to reverse it (mountain to valley, or vice versa)?

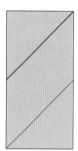

Infinite

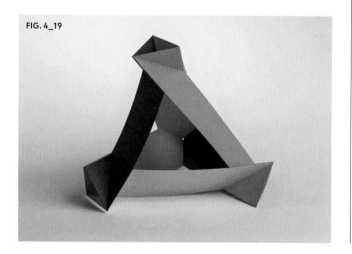

FIG. 4_19

FIG. 4_20

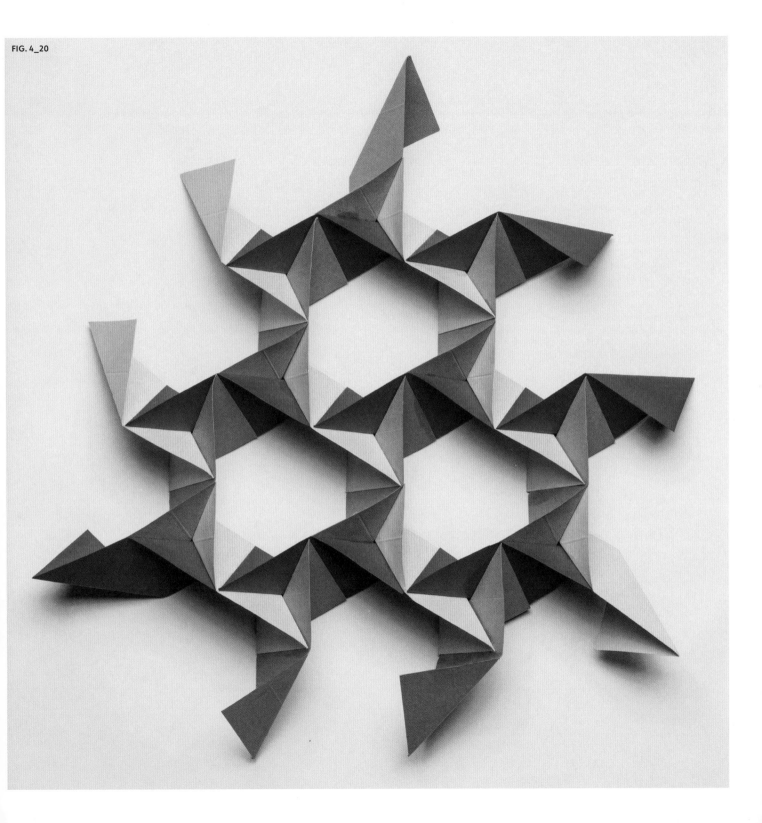

4.5.7
Infinite spiral

Stacks of 45° diagonal folds will create an
infinite chain of spiralling triangles. The form
is immensely strong, much stronger than an
untwisted triangular tube. Its party trick is to roll
down a slope. Hung from the centre point inside
one end, it will spin beautifully in a slight breeze
or in the warm air above a heating unit.

Can it be made from one piece of
card or paper?

Can different sections have different angles?

Can some of the folds be rotated to the other
diagonal?

Can the angles be changed so that the
cross-section is not triangular, but a square,
pentagon or hexagon? Read section
2.3 for tips.

FIG. 4_21

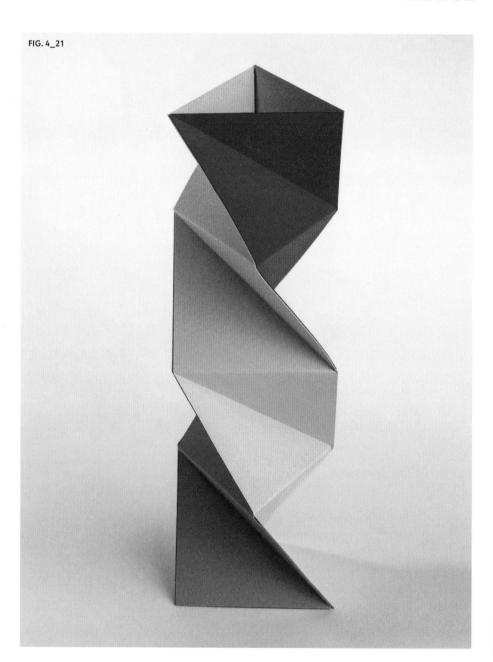

If you have read through the book and made as many of the examples as you have had time to, congratulations! This is definitely one of those books that will repay over and over the time spent studying from it and with it. On the other hand, if you have skimmed it, you have probably learned about three-dimensional symmetry, but not experienced it. If you have the time and motivation, consider making more examples. There really is no substitute for making, making, making. Understanding comes from making, not from looking at images.

If you have grasped the essentials of thinking and designing in the third dimension by making the exercises, your thinking skills and your vocabulary of form as a designer (or however you define your interest, practice or profession) will forever have been expanded. This has to be a good thing. You now have more options to select from and a better sense of how a *whole* three-dimensional form will look, not just of the form as a series of flat views from different angles. This means that your control of surface, space and form will become more complex, more interesting and more sophisticated, giving what you make an intrigue and eliciting from users added appreciation of your work.

This has been a book of exercises to help you think and design in the third dimension. It was not a book of design ideas (although some may incidentally be useful). Your task now, armed with a new design skill, is to use it, away from the book. With your safety net removed, you might struggle at first to apply what you have learned, but with patience and practice, you will improve. Thinking and designing in the third dimension is a muscle that strengthens with practice, over time.

Enjoy your continuing journey into, through, over and around the third dimension. Keep practising. Keep failing. Keep learning. Keep succeeding. As I say to my students, 'Be amazing!'

'Don't just say that you have read books. Show that through them you have learned to think better.'

Epictetus (55–c.135 CE)

Acknowledgements

I wish to thank my students from many design specialities, in many universities, colleges and schools of design over a great many years, for their patience while I tried to understand what designing in the third dimension really meant, by imposing upon them a series of making exercises, with greater or lesser success. Through trial and error, their reactions to these exercises laid the foundations for this book. What now seems to be a clear idea took many years to come into focus through these many exercises, experiments and iterations.

I must thank my editor, Kara Hattersley-Smith, for taking it on trust that my mostly hard-to-grasp concept was worth her time, skill and energy; Alex Coco, for his superb eye for clear and inspirational layouts; Rosie Fairhead for her meticulous copy-editing; Meidad Suchowolski for his luminous photography; and Yoram Ron for his clear, to-the-point videos. The author's name is on the cover, but a book is only as good as the team who make it. I must also thank Color Tree Ltd (www.colortreelimited.co.uk), online retailers of high-quality papers, products and books for papercrafts and origami, for generously sponsoring the card used in the book.

Finally, I must thank my wife, Miri Golan, for her understanding. Part way through writing the book, we won a major award for our ed. tech start-up company. Rather than follow up on the success, she recognized that I needed to complete the book and willingly released me from many of our post-award duties...to which I must now return in haste.

LAURENCE KING

First published in Great Britain in 2024 by
Laurence King
An imprint of Quercus Editions Ltd
Carmelite House
50 Victoria Embankment
London EC4Y 0DZ

An Hachette UK company

A CIP catalogue record for this book is available from the British Library.

PB ISBN 978-1-52943-204-6
Ebook ISBN 978-1-52943-205-3

Quercus Editions Ltd hereby exclude all liability to the extent permitted by law for any errors or omissions in this book and for any loss, damage or expense (whether direct or indirect) suffered by a third party relying on any information contained in this book.

10 9 8 7 6 5 4 3 2 1

Commissioning editor: Kara Hattersley-Smith
Book and cover design by Alexandre Coco
Photography by Meidad Suchowolski
Videos by Yoram Ron
Project manager: Rosanna Fairhead

Printed and bound in China by C&C Offset Printing Co., Ltd.

Papers used by Quercus are from well-managed forests and other responsible sources.